TEACHING MUSIC

Beer and Hoffman

TEACHING MUSIC

Alice S. Beer

Mary E. Hoffman

SILVER BURDETT COMPANY
Morristown, New Jersey
Glenview, Ill. · San Carlos, Calif. · Dallas · Atlanta · Agincourt, Ontario

Cover: Frank Pietrucha

TEACHING MUSIC

Portions of this book are from *Teaching Music: What, How, Why*, © 1973, General Learning Corporation.

ISBN 0-382-05867-4

CONTENTS

Music 31.²⁰ OP

PREFACE

Teaching Music is intended to be used by those who are already teaching music and by students who are preparing to teach music in the elementary school. It gives practical suggestions about what to teach and how. It involves the reader in various teaching processes — analyzing, questioning, assessing, and formulating general principles that will serve as guidelines in new situations. The organization of the book is based on a process of moving from the specific and concrete to the general and abstract.

Teaching Music specifies an objective at the beginning of Chapters 1–11. Each objective defines a skill that is generally accepted as important to successful teaching. Tasks, thought-provoking questions, assignments, and assessments suggest how the objective can be accomplished.

The WHAT section of *Teaching Music* gives concrete examples of teaching procedures for elementary classes, showing how even the youngest children can begin to perceive, conceptualize, analyze, create, and evaluate music by engaging in simple activities — singing, playing, listening, and moving. These sample strategies contain many suggestions to the teacher. Examples of classroom dialogue are provided, printed in green; answers to questions posed in the strategies are enclosed in parentheses. Some of the teaching procedures described, especially those designed for older children, will require at least one class period. Most procedures are intended to comprise only a portion of the usual twenty- or thirty-minute period.

The HOW section of *Teaching Music* involves the reader in identifying, analyzing, and experimenting with a variety of ways to present music to children and involve them in musical responses. Although the examples and illustrations are music-oriented, the information about planning for instruction, group activities, individualized instruction, teacher-student relationships, discipline, and evaluation is applicable to virtually all teaching situations. This section also includes a brief description of methods and approaches that have influenced the teaching of music.

The WHY section of *Teaching Music* briefly examines the functions of the arts in human experience and focuses on those aspects of the arts, particularly music, that make them unique among the academic disciplines. The section encourages the reader to search out his or her own answers to the question "Why do we teach music?"

The authors of *Teaching Music* believe that the musical experience should dominate each methods class session and each in-service workshop. To provide for this, more than 40 songs are scattered throughout the book. Two LP records were made especially to accompany the text.

1

What Will You Teach Six- and Seven-Year-Olds?

CHAPTER OBJECTIVE

Write a teaching procedure that focuses on one inherent quality of music. The teaching procedure should

(a) include at least three of the following activities: singing, playing rhythm or melody instruments, listening, moving, creating;

(b) be suitable for six- and seven-year-olds; and

(c) provide for different levels of ability within the class.

As the teacher, you will have the pivotal role in determining what comprises the music program in your classroom. Will it be songs? Skills? Instrument recognition? Theme recognition? Theory? Certainly all these should be a part of your music program, but none of them should be its ultimate goal. Songs, skill development, and other music activities should be the means of helping your students achieve the chief goal of a school music program — to perceive the inner workings of music. Once students understand basic musical concepts[1] (e.g., fast and slow, upward and downward, beat and no beat), they can apply what they know to all types of music and begin to make their own discoveries and decisions about music. In order to perceive qualities that are inherent in music and understand how they work together, children must experience music.

STRATEGY 1   Here is a sample strategy designed to focus on one aspect of steady beat.

> **Musical movement can be organized into steady beats.**

- We are going to play a game. Look around you and find a space where you can walk without bumping into anything.

If space is limited, it may be necessary to have groups of students take turns playing the game; or the class may walk in a large circle.[2]

---

[1]See Musical Concepts, p. 185.

[2]See Hints for Teaching Movement, p. 190.

- Listen to the words of this song to find when you should walk "all around the kitchen" and when you should "stop right still."

ALL AROUND THE KITCHEN

BLACK-AMERICAN PLAY SONG

TRANSCRIBED AND ADAPTED FROM THE LIBRARY OF CONGRESS FIELD RECORDING AFS 88

All a - round the kit - chen, Cock - a - doo - dle, doo - dle, doo.

All a - round the kit - chen, Cock - a - doo - dle, doo - dle, doo.

Now__ stop right still, Cock - a - doo - dle, doo - dle, doo.

Put your hand on your hip, Cock - a - doo - dle, doo - dle, doo.

Let your right foot slip, Cock - a - doo - dle, doo - dle, doo.

Then__ do it like this, Cock - a - doo - dle, doo - dle, doo.

All a - round the kit - chen, Cock - a - doo - dle, doo - dle, doo.

All a - round the kit - chen, Cock - a - doo - dle, doo - dle, doo.

- Did the words tell you to do something else? ("Put your hand on your hip" and "let your right foot slip")

Repeat the song until most students are acting out the words. On "do it like this," model a different motion each time the song is repeated to give students ideas for creating their own motions later.

Observe students who cannot walk to the steady beat. Give additional practice by having those students walk in a large circle while the class sings the song. As they walk, play a drum accompaniment, keeping time with their beat.

Play this game on different days for a change of pace. Emphasize the steady beat with a light drum accompaniment to help those who have trouble hearing it.

Have students use what they have learned about steady beat in another piece of music:

The Perails: "Boss Walk" (excerpt), Al White and His Hi-Liters

- Listen to this music. Without getting out of your seat, move a hand, foot, or some other part of your body with the music.

Notice students who are keeping the steady beat. Ask only those students to find a space in the room where they can move freely, as you play the recording again.

- On your way back to your seat, please pick up an instrument from the table.

On the table, have instruments of only one type (for example, all wood, all metal, or all drums). This will help students perceive similarity in the tone color of rhythm instruments made of like materials, and it will produce a more musical, less cluttered sound.

- If you have not had a turn to move, you may now find a space where you will not bump into anyone.
- Students in your seats, please play your instruments.

Strategy 1 should be one part of a series of lessons that focus on the concept that music can have a steady beat. It takes into account three important factors in determining what to teach six- and seven-year-olds.

(1) It focuses on one inherent quality of the music, or one concept. This focus is achieved by having students walk to the music. (Walking usually has a natural rhythm that resembles a steady beat.) Both pieces of music used in Strategy 1 have been chosen because of their obvious beat. The beat is brought into the foreground by playing it lightly on a drum, with the recording.

(2) The strategy takes into consideration the maturation level of most young children. Movement, especially large muscle movement, is a fundamental mode of learning and a fundamental mode of expression for young children. Movement aids in developing the physical skills necessary for playing instruments. Growing muscles need to stretch, and movement in music class helps to meet that need.

(3) Strategy 1 provides for a range of physical and musical abilities. Differing levels of ability are found in every class, and the teacher must provide for them. In this strategy, children are directed to walk to the music and then encouraged to respond with a movement of their choice. Extra practice is given to the less mature children, and the beat is changed to match their tempo. The more advanced children are allowed to play instruments. Using instruments of only one tone color introduces the children to the characteristic sound of those instruments. As a result, musically ad-

vanced children will store up the memory of that particular sound. If many types of instruments had been used, no one characteristic sound would have been predominant.

STRATEGY 2   The ability to conceptualize grows out of perceiving the expressive qualities of music and hearing how they work within it. These qualities — rhythm, melody, dynamics, and form, for example — are the basis for musical perceptions. Strategy 1 focuses on steady beat, a concept about rhythm. Strategy 2 focuses on tone color.

> **The sound of each instrument or voice is distinctive.**

- Listen to this song. Maybe what happens in this song happens at your house also.

SOMEBODY'S KNOCKING AT YOUR DOOR

Some-bod-y's knock-ing at your door,

Some-bod-y's knock-ing at your door,

O,___ { Josh - ua, Mar - tha, } why don't you an - swer?

Some-bod-y's knock-ing at your door.___

- Imagine the sound you would hear if someone were knocking at your door. Can you think of an instrument you could play to make that sound? (Wood block, temple block, or other instrument made of wood)

Have one student choose an instrument and play it.

- Does it sound like knocking? (Yes)
- Listen to the song again and play the instrument each time you hear the word *door*.

Have other class members pretend to play.

- Is there another way people let you know they are at the door? (Ring the doorbell)

- If I change the words to "Somebody's ringing at my door," what instrument would you choose? (Triangle, tambourine, or other instrument that can make a ringing sound)
- Listen again and play the triangle on the word *door*.

Have other class members pretend to play.

- Some doorbells have a different sound. They chime. Can you think of an instrument that sounds like that kind of doorbell? (Resonator bells — E and the C# below it, for example)
- Listen to the song again and play the resonator bells.

Use the correct name for each rhythm instrument consistently. Insist that students learn correct names and pronunciations.

Remind students to play rhythm instruments as though they are lifting their hands from a hot stove.

Use what has been learned by playing this game:

- We are going to play the Instrument Game. Even though you cannot see which instrument I'm playing, tell me whether it is made of wood, like the one for knocking at the door.
- Since Jennifer answered correctly, she may choose and play an instrument.
- Is it made of wood or metal?

Play this game as part of several lessons, until most students are able to recognize the instruments by their sound. As students learn the names of the instruments, have them identify each instrument by name (triangle) rather than by broad category (metal).

As students learn to recognize the distinctive sounds of instruments they hear and play in music class, introduce less familiar instruments. Invite older students, teachers, or residents of the community to demonstrate instruments with different tone colors, such as piano, trumpet, clarinet, string bass, and temple block. As a preparation for the following activity, have students observe and pantomime the playing of each instrument that is demonstrated.

The Sounds of Instruments, No. 2

- Here is a picture of an instrument that Mr. Jones played for us yesterday. Suppose you had one right here. Show how you would play it.
- What is the name of the instrument?

Review the names of several instruments and the manner of playing them.

- Listen to this recording. When you hear each instrument, pretend that you are playing it.

Repeat the instrument demonstration if necessary.

Strategy 2 illustrates three factors that should be considered in deciding what to teach six- and seven-year-olds.

(1) The objective centers on increasing students' ability to perceive differences in tone color. The students are required to react to different sounds by recalling and naming familiar environmental sounds (doorbell, etc.), by reproducing those sounds (selecting and playing rhythm instru-

ments), by recognizing and naming instruments when both seen and heard, and finally by recognizing and naming instruments when only heard.

(2) The strategy is suitable for young children, since they not only listen but are expected to demonstrate their level of perception through activity rather than description.[3] Furthermore, the illustrative material is suitable for young children in that sounds to be recognized are singled out and placed in the foreground, without the distraction of background sounds.

(3) The strategy takes into consideration a range of musical and physical abilities found within a class by permitting more advanced students to act as leader in the rhythm instrument game and by providing for both verbal and physical responses.

STRATEGY 3   To help students perceive musical elements more precisely, strategies are designed to focus attention on a specific aspect of an element. Strategy 1 deals with one aspect of rhythm. Strategy 3 stresses the perception of another aspect of rhythm:

> A rhythm pattern is a recognizable combination of long and short sounds.

- Listen to this song.

SING HALLELU   BLACK SPIRITUAL FROM SOUTH CAROLINA

1. Down in the val - ley, Sing hal - le - lu.
2. Mary had a ba - by, Sing hal - le - lu.

Down in the val - ley, Sing hal - le - lu.
Mary had a ba - by, Sing hal - le - lu.

Down in the val - ley, Sing hal - le - lu.
Mary had a ba - by, Sing hal - le - lu.

Down in the val - ley, Sing hal - le - lu.
Mary had a ba - by, Sing hal - le - lu.

---

[3]See Theories of Child Growth and Development, p. 195.

- What words do you hear repeated over and over? ("Sing hallelu")

Sing or play the recording of the song several times so that students become familiar with it. Each time the phrase "sing hallelu" occurs, play a light accompaniment on the tambourine:

Sing hal - le - lu
tap shake tap shake

- This time sing along with the repeated phrase.

Sing two verses without the tambourine. Isolate and practice the phrase as needed.

- This time clap the repeated phrase.

Sing only one verse, playing the tambourine to highlight the rhythm pattern.

- Did you clap the same pattern each time? (Yes)
- How many times did you clap the repeated phrase? (Four times)
- We are going to play follow the leader. Watch closely:

The first time the phrase "sing hallelu" occurs, clap. The second time "sing hallelu" occurs, slap your chest. The third time it occurs, slap your thighs. The fourth time, stamp your feet.

For additional practice, divide the class into four groups. Assign a motion to each group. On another occasion, have students select a different rhythm instrument to play each time the pattern occurs. To add interest and enhance the learning, omit singing on this phrase and listen to the instruments.

To review the learning in a different way, assign resonator bells to four students: The A bell to be played on the first "sing hallelu," G on the second, F on the third, and D on the fourth. Alternate bells and rhythm instruments as the six verses are sung.

The following activity is designed to challenge students to make up and play their own rhythm patterns. This is another way to sharpen their perception of rhythm patterns.

- We are going to play follow the leader. Watch closely. Please stand.

Lead the class in marking time in place. Continue for eight beats. Without breaking rhythm, start to sing "Hambone" (page 8).

Continue marking the steady beat with your feet throughout, as follows:

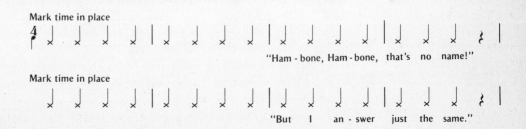

Mark time in place

"Ham - bone, Ham - bone, that's no name!"

Mark time in place

"But I an - swer just the same."

HAMBONE

AFRO-AMERICAN GAME SONG   WORDS BY CARMINO RAVOSA

USED BY PERMISSION.

Group 1   Group 2

1. "Ham-bone, Ham-bone, That's no name!"   (Clap)
2. "Ham-bone, Ham-bone, got big feet!"   (Clap)

Group 1   Group 2

"But   I   an-swer just the same."   (Clap)
"They still get me 'cross the street."   (Clap)

3. "Hambone, Hambone, got no brain!" (Clap)

"Still I keep out of the rain." (Clap)

4. "Hambone, Hambone, where you been?" (Clap)

"Round the world and back again!" (Clap)

5. "Hambone, Hambone, don't cha smile?" (Clap)

"Ev'ry little once in a while!" (Clap)

6. "Hambone, Hambone, don't cha cry?" (Clap)

"When I get somethin' in my eye!" (Clap)

If students begin to sing along, silence them by putting your finger to your lips. It is most important that students hear the song several times before attempting to sing. Sing two or three verses, more if attention has not wandered. Do not break the rhythm, and do not allow the tempo to quicken.

- Stop. Did you notice that your feet kept a steady beat all the way through? Listen to this recording. Do you hear a part that is *not* a steady beat? (Yes, when the singer stops)
- Raise your hand when you hear the part that is *not* a steady beat.
- Clap a rhythm that is *not* a steady beat each time the singer stops.

Usually some students will clap a rhythm pattern and others will continue to clap the steady beat. Select those students who clap a pattern to form group 2 and those who clap the steady beat to form group 1, as indicated in the music. Observe those students in group 2 who consistently clap a pattern at the appropriate time, and have those individuals take turns clapping their pattern. Have group 1 clap the steady beat.

- Allison, will you clap your pattern for the class.
- Let's all clap Allison's pattern.
- Is Allison's pattern different from the steady beat? (Yes)
- As I play it on the tambourine, listen for some long sounds and some short sounds.
- How did I play the long sounds? (Shook the tambourine)

- Allison, will you play your pattern on the tambourine so that we can all hear the long and short sounds.

Strategy 3 shows additional ways to meet the objectives for Chapter 1.
    (1) The strategy focuses on one inherent quality of music:

> **A rhythm pattern is a recognizable combination of long and short sounds.**

    (2) The activities include singing, playing both melody and rhythm instruments, moving, listening, and creating. Specific activities include reacting to a rhythm pattern in a song by clapping, stamping, etc.; producing a rhythm pattern; differentiating between steady beat (sounds of equal duration) and rhythm patterns (sounds of unequal duration) — or discovering what a rhythm pattern is and what it is not.
    (3) The activities are suitable for young children. They are short and diverse to allow for a short attention span, and they include physical movement. The selection of material is suitable for young children in that songs are short, repetitive, and of limited vocal range. The rhythm patterns are simple and are made obvious by bringing them into the foreground.
    (4) The strategy takes into account a range of musical and physical abilities. Students create rhythm patterns within the level of their own ability. Capable students are given an opportunity to act as leaders. Physical activities range from a simple one, stepping in place, to a more advanced one, involving tapping and shaking a tambourine.

ASSESSMENT 1 You have studied three strategies. Each reflects the chapter objectives and includes several types of activities. Each activity (1) focuses on one inherent quality of music, (2) involves singing and playing, (3) uses materials and activities suitable to the maturation level of six- and seven-year-olds, and (4) provides for a range of ability levels.
    Strategy 4, like the other strategies, illustrates the same factors; however, *you* are expected to decide: (1) what concept is being taught, (2) what activities bring about the learning, (3) how provision is made for a range of developmental levels, and (4) why the activities are suitable for six- and seven-year-olds.

STRATEGY 4
- This song tells about doing two things. Listen and find out what they are.

I'M GONNA SING   BLACK SPIRITUAL

I'm gon - na {sing / pray} when the spi - rit says {"sing," / "pray,"} _____

And o - bey the spi - rit of the Lord. _____

- How are the two verses sung differently? (One loud, one soft)
- Now, look on this side of the room. You see a picture of a big steam shovel. Does a steam shovel make a loud sound, or a soft sound? (Loud)
- Look on the other side of the room. Do you see a picture of something that makes a soft sound? (Pictures of a boy fishing, a kitten, etc.)
- Listen to the song again and point to the picture that tells whether the music is soft or loud. (The first stanza is loud, the second is soft.)

Call for responses that enable you to assess the level of understanding of all students.

- Listen to the words. *Why* is one verse loud and the other soft? (A prayer is usually said softly.)
- Listen as I sing one part. Is it the loud part, or the soft part? (Loud part)
- Sing the loud part with me. Ready, sing.
- Your loud part is very good, now sing the soft part after me.
- Today we are going to play a game. Take your place in the large circle.
- Start to walk when you hear the drum. Stop when the drum stops.

Play the drum loudly in a steady walking tempo.

- Listen carefully. If the sound of the drum changes, walk in a different way.

Play several measures of loud beats, followed by several measures of soft beats. Praise those who show the difference in loud and soft by the way they walk.

- Today we are going to play a bell part with the song. Pretend you have a bell just like mine and copy what I do. Remember to match your bell playing to the loud and soft parts.

Demonstrate playing the G bell on the first beat of each measure. Observe students who successfully show soft and loud by the vigor of their motions. Select them to play the bells. If there are some mature students in the group, assign bells in the G chord (G,B,D) to some and bells in the D chord (D,F#,A,C) to others. Have them play the appropriate chord on the first beat of each measure. Have the class evaluate the players' ability to play soft and loud sounds at the appropriate times.

<pre>
              G   G
I'm gonna SING when the spirit says "SING,"
              G   D₇
I'm gonna SING when the spirit says "SING,"
              G   G
I'm gonna SING when the spirit says "SING,"
       D₇   G
And o-BEY the spirit of the LORD.
</pre>

The following activity challenges students to use what they have learned by making some musical decisions of their own.

- Listen to this song. Can you choose a word to tell what the feeling of the song is? (Sleepy, quiet, etc.)

ALL NIGHT, ALL DAY   BLACK-AMERICAN FOLK SONG

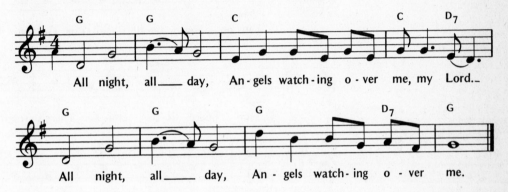

Accept responses without comment. Children should begin to realize that people respond differently to music. However, the words of this song give a clue to its meaning, and consequently a clue to how it should be performed.

- Listen again. What is this song about? (Angels watching over me)
- Listen again. When do the angels watch over me? (All night, all day)
- If this song were sung at night to put you to sleep, what would it be called? (A lullaby)
- Listen to the song sung two ways.

Sing first loudly and then softly. If you use the recording, change the volume control to make the second part of the music softer.

- Which way do you think would be best for a lullaby? (Second way)
- Why? (It must be sung softly if it is a lullaby.)
- How do you think we should sing this song, soft or loud? (Softly)
- Did we sing it softly?
- If we were singing this to put a baby to sleep and the baby fell asleep before we finished the song, what do you think we would do? (Get softer toward the end)
- Let's sing it that way.

ASSESSMENT 2   In Assessment 1 you were asked to study Strategy 4 and deduce (1) the concept, (2) why the activities were suitable for young children, and (3) the means by which a range of levels of ability were provided for.

Assessment 2 will give you the concept and the music. You are to (1) supply activities that focus on the concept, (2) explain why they are suitable for the age level, and (3) identify ways in which the different abilities within the class are provided for.

The concept you are to work with has to do with form, specifically this:

> Music can be organized into sections that are alike or different.

The suggested music is:

GET ON BOARD   BLACK SPIRITUAL

Get on board, lit-tle chil-dren, Get on board, lit-tle chil-dren,

Fine

Get on board, lit-tle chil-dren, There's room for man-y a more.

The gos-pel train's a-com-ing. I hear it close at hand,____

D.C. al Fine

I hear the car-wheels rum-bling And roll-ing through the land.

Study Music Concepts (page 185), Theories of Child Growth and Development (page 195), and the music found throughout this book. Plan a procedure that (1) focuses on an inherent quality in the music; (2) shows how this quality can be taught through at least three of the following activities: singing, playing rhythm or melody instruments, listening, moving, creating; (3) is suitable for six- and seven-year-olds; and (4) provides for a range of levels of ability within the class.

2

What Will You Teach Seven-, Eight-, and Nine-Year-Olds?

CHAPTER OBJECTIVE

Write a teaching procedure that focuses on one inherent quality of music. The procedure should

(a) *provide for an increasing sensitivity to music;*

(b) *take into account the maturation of the students; and*

(c) *include the use of one of the following: recorder, melody bells, concrete objects, or visual aids.*

When students reach the age of seven, eight, or nine years and are in what has traditionally been known as third and fourth grades, they should be challenged to perceive and react to more complexities in the music and to more complex musical concepts. They should be refining skills in performing and reacting to music. In Chapter 1, this perception about rhythm was discussed:

> **A rhythm pattern is a recognizable combination of long and short sounds.**

The following strategy builds on that perception and makes it more complex by adding another dimension:

> **More than one pattern of short and long sounds can occur together.**

STRATEGY 5   Teachers often use the rhythms of a familiar song to show how rhythm patterns can occur together. Teach "Sambalele" by rote.[1]

---

[1]See Generalizations on Teaching Rote Songs, p. 187.

SAMBALELE

FOLK SONG FROM BRAZIL   WORDS BY RUTH AND THOMAS MARTIN

1. Hear how   the   mu - sic   is   play - ing,
2. Dance while   the   drum - beat   is   pound - ing,

Dance   to   its   light - heart - ed   mea - sures,
Mel - low   gui - tars   soft - ly   strum - ming,

Clap - ping   and   stamp - ing   and   sway - ing,
And   cas - ta - nets   clear - ly   sound - ing,

Join   in   the   car - ni - val   plea - sures.
Join   in   the   whis - tling   and   hum - ming.

B REFRAIN

Sam - ba,   sam - ba,   sam - ba - la - le - le,

While   we   are   danc - ing   and   sing - ing   so   gai - ly,

Sam - ba,   sam - ba,   sam - ba - la - le - le,

While   we   are   danc - ing   and   sing - ing   so   gai - ly.

• Slap your thighs in this rhythm, chanting[2] as you slap:

Sam - ba, sam - ba, sam - ba   etc.
L   R   L   R   L   R

[2]See Hints for Teaching Music Reading, p. 188.

When most students can clap the pattern, use it as an accompaniment to the refrain. Have successful students play the pattern on bongo drums.

Make a visual aid[3] that is an accurate representation of the short and long sounds. If possible, make the visual aid from something that can be manipulated by students. For example, cut pieces of construction paper in lengths that accurately show the duration of eighth and quarter notes. Make the quarter notes twice as long as the eighth notes. These can be fastened to the chalkboard or bulletin board with masking tape and easily manipulated. This is how the pattern from "Sambalele" would look.

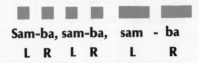

Sam-ba, sam-ba,   sam - ba
  L   R   L   R   L   R

Use pieces of construction paper to form other rhythm patterns.

- You played the pattern very well. How would it sound if it were backward?

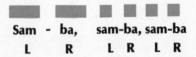

Sam - ba,   sam-ba, sam-ba
 L   R   L R L R

When the pattern has been mastered, have a student play it on the claves. Have the class sing the entire song as the two patterns are played.

Repeat throughout the verse only:

Claves  etc.

Repeat throughout the refrain only:

Bongos etc.

To further clarify the learning experience, have the class clap the rhythm of the words in addition to the claves and bongo parts suggested above. To bring the two simultaneous patterns into the foreground, eliminate the singing, leaving only the sound of the patterns played by the instruments, and the rhythm of the melody:

[3]See Hints for Teaching Music Reading, p. 188.

Verse:

Refrain:

When the rhythm played on the bongos is mastered, individuals can learn to play a bell part on their own. They will need a set of bells with letter names marked on them, a place to work, and time for individual practice. The part can be played throughout the song or on the refrain only. If bells of different tone colors or different octaves are available, alternate them on verse and refrain for added interest.

The medium of music is sound. As students learn to differentiate sounds, they will progress in their musical development. Test students' ability to hear repeated rhythm patterns in another setting.

🎯 **Anonymous: Coranto**

- **We have been working with patterns that happen together. Can you hear a pattern that is repeated over and over in this music? (A tambourine plays this pattern throughout.)**

If students have trouble hearing the pattern, bring it into the foreground by clapping it lightly as you play the recording again.

- **When you hear the repeated pattern, clap it with the recording.**
- **On the chalkboard you can show the long and short sounds in the pattern you just clapped. As you listen and clap the pattern again, decide how it should be shown.**

Have students manipulate the visual materials to represent the pattern. It should look like this.

Test the ways in which students form the pattern by clapping them and saying the words *long* and *short*. Continue until the correct representation is made. Add standard notation to the representation. Eventually use only standard notation.

Have students discover long and short patterns in the classroom, in their clothing, and on the playground. Display a variety of paintings or photographs to explore the many ways other art forms use patterns. Invite the art teacher's participation.

STRATEGY 6 To learn more about the inner workings of music, students need many opportunities to perceive musical elements. This will not happen unless the teacher plans ways to focus attention on specific characteristics such as melodic direction.

> Tones move upward and downward, creating a sense of direction.

BROTHER NOAH AMERICAN SEA SONG

REPRINTED FROM AMERICAN SEA SONGS AND CHANTEYS. COMPILED BY FRANK SHAY AND ILLUSTRATED BY EDWARD A. WILSON. BY PERMISSION OF W. W. NORTON & COMPANY. INC. COPYRIGHT 1948 BY FRANK SHAY AND EDWARD A. WILSON. COPYRIGHT RENEWED 1976.

1. Broth-er No-ah, Broth-er No-ah,
2. No, you can't, sir, No, you can't, sir,

May I come in-to the Ark of the Lord,
You can't come in-to the Ark of the Lord,

For it's grow-ing ver-y dark and it's rain-ing ver-y hard?
Though it's grow-ing ver-y dark and it's rain-ing ver-y hard.

REFRAIN

Hal-le-loo, hal-le-loo, hal-le-loo-oo-oo-oo-ia!

- Look at the music as you listen to "Brother Noah." Follow the notes with your eyes. Is anything missing in the music? (Yes. There are no notes at the end of the song.)
- Listen again. Do the missing notes go up, or down? (Down)
- Look at these two melodies.

1. D C B A G

2. G A B C D

- Which one is the missing part of the song? (Number 1)
- Let's use our ears to test it. Look at the bells. Notice the letter names on them. Match those letter names with the letter names on the music. Play number 1. Now play number 2. Which is the missing part? (Number 1)

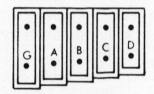

- Listen to this part of the melody. Is it number 1, or number 2, or neither?

Sing the phrase "I come into the Ark of the Lord." (It is neither melody. It stays on the same tone.)

- Look at your music book, and find the phrase I just sang. Do the notes go upward, or downward, or stay the same? (They stay the same.) We call them repeated tones.
- Who is ready to play the repeated tones on the bells? Use the rhythm of the words "I come into the Ark of the Lord."
- Can you find another place where the tune has repeated tones? ("growing very dark and it's raining very hard")
- Who is ready to play those repeated tones on the bells? Use the A bell to play "growing very dark and it's raining very hard."

Direct students to find a space in the room where they can swing their arms without bumping into each other.

- When you hear the bells play the part that stays on one tone, show with your arms how that part goes. Show by moving in a different way when you hear the part that moves downward. Move only your arms. Move only when the bells play.

If space is limited, have students stand and clap the rhythm of the repeated tones, keeping their hands at one level. Have them move their hands from high to low as they clap the rhythm of the pattern that goes downward. It will be helpful to practice the clapping activity first with bells only, then with the recording and the bells, and finally with the recording only.

The procedure above deals with identifying a short melodic fragment that moves in a downward direction as opposed to one with repeated tones. The following procedure deals with a more complex idea about upward and downward direction. The musical setting is also more complex.

HAND ME DOWN

Teach the song by rote. The procedure should include listening at least three times. Each time, call for a different response to something in the song, such as finding chorus parts that are alike (choruses one and three, and two and four), clapping on choruses one and three, and stamping on choruses two and four. Then have students sing just the chorus parts.

- Look at these two patterns. How are they different? (One moves upward and the other downward.)

Play pattern 1 and have students tell which pattern is being played. Play each pattern as many times as necessary for most students to see the relationship between the sound and the notation.

- Look at number 3. How is it different from number 1 and number 2? (It combines numbers 1 and 2.)

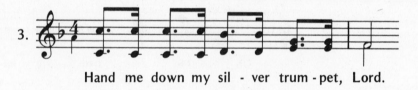

- How will the sound be different? (Both parts will be sung at the same time.)
- David, you have learned to play the bells very well. Will you play number 1? Bruce, will you stand beside David so that you can learn to play it too?

Have children work together as often as possible. Children learn from each other.

Call on another capable student to play pattern 2. If bells are not available, the piano can be used. Be sure to call students' attention to the notation as the parts are played.

Divide the students into two groups.

- David, will you stand in front of group 1? Play your bell part with the group as they sing it.

Follow the same procedure for playing and singing pattern 2. Finally, have the two groups sing simultaneously. Practice until the two groups sing with confidence. If students can play G, A, C, and D on the recorder, introduce an easy echo part.

Have students determine whether the echo parts move in an upward or a downward direction. In addition, lead them to discover the repeated tones in the first and third chorus parts.

Often a song such as "Hand Me Down" can be used again and again to serve the purpose of a particular lesson. Each time a piece is reviewed, a new activity should be introduced, new learning should result, or previous learning should be reinforced. The activities just described would comprise parts of several lessons.

The teacher faces the problem of matching the developmental levels of students grouped together in a class with the music, with the concept, and with the level of difficulty of the musical skills being taught. There are at least two positive actions the teacher can take:

1. Plan each lesson to provide for a range of abilities, as described in Chapter 1.
2. Plan stepwise progressions, or sequential learning experiences, to give students the necessary background for each new perception and skill.

STRATEGY 7   In Chapter 1 there is a strategy designed to help students perceive that music can have a steady beat. That strategy is one stepping stone for more difficult perceptions about rhythm. The following strategy shows one way to play a stepwise progression toward the realization of a more complex perception about rhythm:

Beats can be organized into sets of two or three.

GING GONG GOOLI

FOLK SONG FROM BRITISH GUIANA

Ging gong goo-li goo-li goo-li goo-li wat-cha,

Ging gong goo, ging gong goo.

Ging gong goo-li goo-li goo-li goo-li wat-cha,

Ging gong goo, ging gong goo.

Hai - la, _____ hai - la shai - la, _____

Shai - la hai - la shai - la ho - la - ho!

Hai - la, _____ hai - la shai - la, _____

Shai - la hai - la shai - la ho! _____

• **Stand and follow my motions.**

Demonstrate a set of motions in sets of two, such as

> Slap thighs, clap
> or
> Clap, snap
> or
> Push right arm forward, push left arm forward
> or
> Stamp, clap

Give clear directions for starting and stopping. If the class tends to get faster, stop and start again. Here is a suggested sequence. Say the words as you demonstrate the motions.

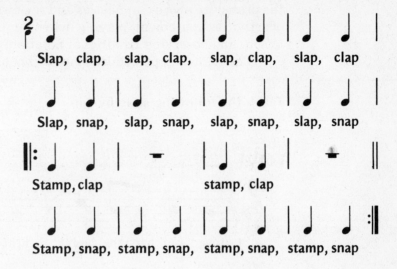

Play the recording of "Ging Gong Gooli" (record 1) and model the motions suggested above in time to the music. Observe students and choose capable ones to lead the class in their own original motions. Play the recording again. While the music plays, make a simultaneous visual aid by drawing beat marks on the chalkboard in time with the music.

- Look at the beat marks on the chalkboard. Some are taller and some are shorter. Beat 1 in each set is shown by a taller mark. Beat 2 in each set is shorter.
- If you were choosing instruments to play with the recording, would you choose a loud or a soft instrument to play on the taller marks? (Loud) What instrument would you choose? (A drum or cymbals, or some other instrument with a loud sound)
- What instrument would you choose to play the shorter marks? (One that would not sound as loud, such as a wood block)
- Let's play the instruments you have chosen as John points to the beat marks on the chalkboard.

Write the pattern on the chalkboard using traditional notation.

- Here is a pattern that uses the sounds we just heard.

Call students' attention to the 2 in the meter signature. Explain that the 2 means that there are two beats in each set, or measure.

Students will have had many experiences with beats in sets of two; however, the procedure above emphasizes and reviews the learning through a range of activities: movement, playing instruments, producing a visual representation, and observing traditional notation.

The following procedure emphasizes beats in sets of three.

Teach the following song by rote.

LOVE   WORDS AND MUSIC BY CARMINO · RAVOSA   © 1971 CARMINO RAVOSA

1. Love can charm the birds___ right out of the trees,

Love can take the hon - ey a - way from the bees;

Love can make a li - on stand up and say, "Please."___

2. Love can turn a hurricane into a breeze,

   Love can get a hermit to smile and say, "Cheese";

   Love can make a dog learn to live with his fleas.

3. Love can bring a giant right down to his knees,

   Love can make the North and the South Poles unfreeze;

   Love can make a kid learn to eat all his peas.

- Find a place in the room where you can move your arms and shoulders without bumping into anyone or anything. You will not need to move your feet.
- Make large circles with your arms or shoulders, or both. Listen to the music as you move.

When most students' movements show that they feel the stronger first beat of each measure (set), have some students play the triangle or finger cymbals. Have them follow this notation:

When students have mastered this rhythm, they can practice the following recorder[4] or bell part. The bell players will need a set of bells with letter names marked on them, and a time and place to practice. If recorders have been introduced, individuals can practice on their own. They may need a recorder fingering chart.

Call students' attention to the 3 in the meter signature. Make sure they know that the 3 means there are three beats in each measure and that the quarter note below it means that a quarter note lasts for one beat.

This strategy fits into a sequence beginning with procedures that focus on beat/no beat, steady beat, and finally on the organization of beats into two or three meter. The sequence is one way to help students become increasingly competent in dealing with music concepts. Each perception is more complex and more demanding. The music is also somewhat more subtle than the short and obvious music suitable for younger children.

More maturity, both physical and musical, is required in these strategies than in strategies for younger children. The phrases are longer and more sustained, making them harder to sing. Skills in playing recorder and bells are introduced. Steps are taken toward musical literacy by helping students relate sound to symbol (traditional notation).

ASSESSMENT 1
The following activities are designed to build on Strategy 7 in a sequence of learning experiences about beat. After you have studied the activities, answer these questions:

(1) What concept is being taught?
(2) How do the activities provide for the advancement of musical sensitivity? For the maturation of the student?
(3) Is the music more complex than in earlier strategies? In what ways?

_____

[4]See Hints for Teaching Recorder, p. 191.

Lead the class through a series of hand motions. First do each motion twice: Clap-clap/snap-snap/ etc. Then do each motion three times: Clap-clap-clap/snap-snap-snap/ etc. Practice until students can change readily from threes to twos. Repeat as many times as necessary to last throughout the music.

Prepare a visual aid to represent the number of times each motion should be performed:

After the class has learned to follow the visual aid, show how the sounds can be written in traditional notation:

Have students select and play rhythm instruments with contrasting tone colors to show the contrast between meter in two and meter in three.

Teach students the terms *two meter* and *three meter*, explaining the meaning of the top number in the meter signature. Help them discover that the note at the bottom of the meter signature shows what kind of note lasts for one beat.

As they listen to the music, have students look at *Call Chart: Meter* (page 27, record 1).

- Take out paper and pencil. Write four measures of meter in two and four measures of meter in three.
- As we listen again, look at the notes you have written. When you hear meter in two, follow those notes with your eyes. When you hear meter in three, follow the notes that show meter in three.
- Now listen again and tap each beat with your pencil eraser. Tap beats in sets of two, or beats in sets of three.

1 METER IN TWO

2 METER IN THREE

3 METER IN TWO

ASSESSMENT 2 In this chapter you have been led through a series of procedures that illustrate ways in which seven-, eight-, and nine-year-olds can grow in their sensitivity to the inherent qualities of music through activities that are suitable to their level of maturation. These activities include the use of recorder, bells, concrete objects, and visual aids. Here is your assignment:

Write a procedure that (1) focuses on one inherent quality of music and (2) includes the use of recorder, bells, concrete objects, or visual aids. Explain why the procedure is suitable for seven-, eight-, and nine-year-olds.

3

What Will You Teach Nine-, Ten-, and Eleven-Year-Olds?

CHAPTER OBJECTIVE Write a teaching procedure that focuses on one inherent quality of music. The procedure should

(a) include several concepts that center on that one quality;

(b) be able to be divided into several class sessions; and

(c) include at least three of the following activities: singing, playing rhythm instruments, playing melody or harmony instruments, moving, listening, creating.

STRATEGY 8 As children grow in perception, they are able to make more subtle discoveries about music — not only new music, but also music they already know. They become able to deal with concepts in a more diversified way. In previous strategies, students have begun a sequence of experiences dealing with beat as a rhythm concept. In this strategy, they will deal with other concepts about beat.

> **In some music, the beat gets faster, gets slower, or pauses.**

If time permits, review some of the songs that students already know as examples of beat getting faster, getting slower, or pausing.
  Teach "The Drunken Sailor" by rote.[1]

---

[1]See Hints for Teaching Rote Songs, p. 186.

THE DRUNKEN SAILOR CAPSTAN SHANTEY

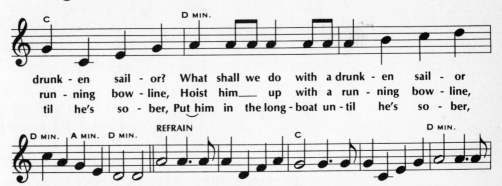

1. What shall we do with a drunk-en sail-or? What shall we do with a
2. Hoist him___ up with a run-ning bow-line, Hoist him___ up with a
3. Put him in the long-boat un-til he's so-ber, Put him in the long-boat un-

drunk-en sail-or? What shall we do with a drunk-en sail-or
run-ning bow-line, Hoist him___ up with a run-ning bow-line,
til he's so-ber, Put him in the long-boat un-til he's so-ber,

REFRAIN

Ear-lye in the morn-ing? Way, hey, and up she ris-es, Way, hey, and up she ris-es, Way, hey, and

up she ris-es Ear-lye in the morn - ing.

4. Pull out the plug and wet him all over, . . .

5. Tie him to the mast until he's sober, . . .

6. That's what we do with a drunken sailor, . . .

Teach these hand motions. When students can do them easily, have them do the motions with the song.

    Pat knees twice
    Clap hands twice
    With palms down, pass the right hand across above the left twice
    With palms down, pass the left hand across above the right twice
    Snap fingers to the left twice
    Snap fingers to the right twice
    "Thumb a ride" over the left shoulder twice
    "Thumb a ride" over the right shoulder twice
    Repeat all the motions above

•   Do the motions help you feel the beat? (Yes)

Lead the class in singing one verse of the song again, this time with slap-snap motions (slap thighs on beat one, snap fingers on beat two). Use the traditional down-up motions for conducting meter in two. Keep the beat steady throughout.

Have students sing the song without the motions as you conduct, slowing down and speeding up your conducting motions. Watch to see how well students follow you.

- You did that very well. Now let's add the slap-snap motions to the singing. I'm going to slow down and speed up in different places, so be sure you are watching carefully.

- What happened to the tempo of your hand motions when the tempo of the song changed? (The motions became slower or faster to match the tempo of the song.)

Show students a symbol for steady beat.

Have the class do the hand motions once through as you point to the beat marks, moving from left to right.

- Are your motions steady? Can you tell when the next motion will happen? (Yes)

Change the symbol for steady beat to show that the beat gets faster.

Have the class do the hand motions once through as you point to the symbol for beat getting faster.

- What happened at the end? (The beats were closer together.) How did you change your hand motions? (The motions became faster.)

- Sing the song again as I point to these beat marks. Where will the song get faster? (At the end of the verse and at the end of the refrain)

- How could you make beat marks to show the beat getting slower? (By making the beat marks farther apart)

Encourage individual students to make beat marks on the chalkboard and to point to the marks as the class sings or does hand motions.

Help the class use what they have learned in a new setting.

- Remember what you know about tempo as you listen to the recording of this song. Find out whether the tempo changes. (No, the tempo stays the same.)

A GREAT BIG SEA

FOLK SONG FROM NEWFOUNDLAND

FROM OLD TIME SONGS AND POETRY OF NEWFOUNDLAND. REPRINTED BY PERMISSION OF GERALD S. DOYLE LTD.

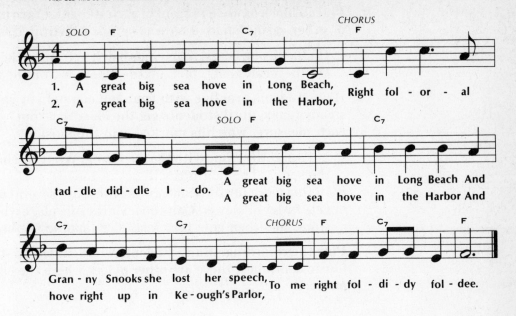

1. A great big sea hove in Long Beach, Right fol-or-al
2. A great big sea hove in the Harbor,

tad-dle did-dle I-do.
A great big sea hove in Long Beach And
A great big sea hove in the Harbor And

Gran-ny Snooks she lost her speech, To me right fol-di-dy fol-dee.
hove right up in Ke-ough's Parlor,

3. "Oh, mother dear, I wants a sack,"   With beads and buttons down the back,"
   Right fol-or-al taddle diddle I-do.   To me right fol-didy fol-dee.
   "Oh, mother dear, I wants a sack

- Sing along with the recording. Make up your own hand motions as you sing. Remember that you will want your motions to happen on the steady beat.
- Sing the first verse of the song without the recording. Think about where we might speed up or slow down the tempo. (The tempo might be changed during the solo parts, for example, and kept steady during the chorus parts for contrast.)

Use the recording to teach the following song.

SASA AKROMA

SINGING GAME FROM AFRICA

FROM AFRICAN SONGS AND GAMES FOR CHILDREN COMPILED AND TRANSCRIBED BY KOJO FOSU BAIDEN AND GERALDINE SLAUGHTER. © 1970. KOJO FOSU BAIDEN AND GERALDINE SLAUGHTER.

Sah   sah kroh mah   woh nay ah   woh chay chay nkoh koh mah.

Sah   sah kroh mah   woh nay ah   woh chay chay nkoh koh mah.

Practice singing the song until students can sing it easily. Then have the students sit on the floor in circles with approximately eight in each circle. Place a block of wood in front of each student. (Yarn balls, sponges, stones, or other easily handled objects can be substituted for blocks of wood.)

- On the strong beats, place your block in front of the player on your right. On the weak beats, pick up the block in front of you.

Have students practice with you. You can help by saying "put-take" in a steady tempo until students get the idea. Say "put" on the strong beat of each measure, which is marked X in the music.

- Let's play the game with the recording. What will happen near the end of the song? (The motions will get faster.)
- In this piece for flute and guitar there are several places where the beat gets faster or slower. Can you hear the one place where the music almost stops, and then gets very fast? Try tapping the beat softly.

Play the recording. Many students will hear the first slight pause. As the music continues, there are other places where the beat slows or seems to pause.

🔊 Ibert, Jacques: Entr'acte for Flute and Guitar

- Does the music get slower in any other places?

This time, play the entire excerpt. There are two other places where the music gets slower. You will need to listen to the music several times before presenting it to the class, so that you can anticipate the places where the beat gets slower. As students listen, you can give them visual cues to indicate that the beat gets slower.

Strategy 8 demonstrates the use of several activities — singing, rhythmic movement, rhythm games, and listening — focused on the perception of steady beat and the ways the beat can change. The lesson moves from the specific (a particular song) to the general (the same musical quality in other songs, games, and listening selections).

STRATEGY 9   With more mature students, there is often a need to expand a teaching strategy to cover more material than can be used in one class session. This strategy has been divided into segments with an indication that the lesson be continued on another day.

> 1. Melodies are ways of organizing pitches.
> 2. Scales are arrangements of tones according to pitch.

Many students will remember the following song. Those who remember it can help the other students learn it.

SHE'LL BE COMIN' ROUND THE MOUNTAIN

SOUTHERN MOUNTAIN SONG

1. She'll be com - in' round the moun - tain when she comes,_____
2. She'll be driv - in' six white hor - ses when she comes,_____

She'll be com - in' round the moun - tain when she comes,_____
She'll be driv - in' six white hor - ses when she comes,_____

She'll be com - in' round the moun - tain,
She'll be driv - in' six white hor - ses,

She'll be com - in' round the moun - tain,
She'll be driv - in' six white hor - ses,

She'll be com - in' round the moun - tain when she comes._____
She'll be driv - in' six white hor - ses when she comes._____

3. Oh, we'll kill the old red rooster when she comes, . . .

4. Oh, we'll all have chicken and dumplings when she comes, . . .

5. Oh, we'll all go out to meet her when she comes, . . .

- Today we're going to add a harmony part to this old song. I will need eight helpers.

Hand out resonator bells for the G-major scale.

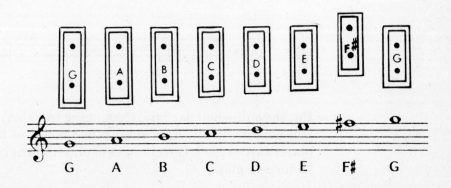

G   A   B   C   D   E   F#   G

So that students in their seats can see, have the students with bells and mallets line up in the order of the scale with G on the left facing the class. This will facilitate matters when other members of the class become the bell players.

- Our bell part is really not very difficult. We'll start with the lowest and largest bell, low G, and play one after another up to the smallest and highest bell, high G. I'll help you keep together by pointing to you when it's your turn to play.

The students will be playing the G-major scale like this:

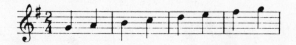

Have the bell players practice this part a few times. Bells begin on the syllable *com-*.

- Let's sing the song while the bell players play their part. The singers will have two notes just before the bells start playing. Watch me, bell players, and I'll help you get started.

As soon as the bells have played their part through once, stop them but encourage the class to keep on singing to the end of the first verse.

- The bells stopped playing because they had come to the end of their part. However, it seems that we haven't finished our part at the same time. How could we make the bell part longer to match the length of the song?

Solicit answers from the class and try their ideas. Some students may suggest repeating the bell part. Others may suggest playing the bell part backward (downward). Both of these are good solutions. One way to accompany the entire verse would be this:

Put the entire bell part and the singing together. Let other students try the bell part while the class sings other verses of the song. Since this many players are needed, two changes of players can give almost the entire class a chance to play.

ANOTHER DAY

Place the bells for the G-major scale in a random order on a table or desk like this:

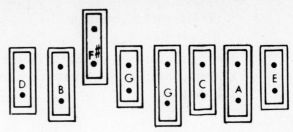

Choose a student to play this series of pitches from left to right and from right to left.

- Does this sound like the beginning of the bell part for "She'll Be Comin' Round the Mountain"? (No)
- Why not? (Students will probably say the sounds should go upward and downward in order, or step by step.)
- Since all the pitches we need for the bell part are here, what do we need to do in order to play the part?

Many of the students will reiterate that the bells will have to be put into upward or downward order. Some students may use such descriptions as "The bells have to go from big to little." This is not incorrect, but encourage students to use their listening ability in determining what to do.

- You can use your ears to decide in what order to put the bells.

Keep the bells in random order as shown above. Give one bell to each of eight students. Have the students face the class in a line across the front of the room. Encourage students to think of this activity as a game.

- Let's find the lowest pitch first. Why would we want to do that? (Because the harmony part to the song starts on the lowest pitch)
- We have to start somewhere. Let's hear the first pitch on the left, D. Now let's listen carefully and see whether this pitch is higher or lower than the next pitch, B. (Higher) Then, which pitch should be moved to the class's left? (B) Why? (Because we are putting the lowest pitches on the left)

Continue in this manner. B is compared with F# and is found to be lower. Eventually, by comparing whatever pitch is at the left of the line of bell players, the lowest pitch (low G) will be discovered.

- We have found the lowest pitch. How can we put the bells in the correct order from low to high by using our listening ability?

Have students alternate low G with each pitch in the line until the class finds the next higher pitch, A. Put A next to G. Now play G and A and find the next pitch, B. Continue until all the pitches are in order from low to high. After all the bells have been placed in the correct order, prove that the problem is solved by playing the bell part with "She'll Be Comin' Round the Mountain."

- We've organized the bells in the right order for playing this song. Does anyone know what we call this ordering of sounds?

Some students may know the term *scale*. If not, this is the time to label the concept. Labeling helps students recall their learning experiences.

Have the students play the scale from low to high and from high to low.

- This is called a major scale. You can make up a melody using the tones of this scale.

Show the students one way to invent a simple melody by pointing to the bell players, one at a time, when you want them to play. An example could be as follows:

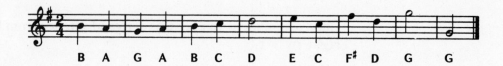

Let several students make up melodies in this manner. Be careful to let students create for themselves. At this point, do not be too strict about rhythm or about ending on the tonal center (G). The purpose of this activity is to help students work with the raw material of melody.

ANOTHER DAY

- Many of the songs we already know use the pitches of the major scale. Here's one you probably already know.

If the class doesn't know "Old Blue," teach it by rote.

OLD BLUE SOUTHERN MOUNTAIN SONG

2. I grabbed my axe and I tooted my horn,
   Gonna git me a 'possum in the new-ground corn. *Refrain*

3. Chased that ol' 'possum up a 'simmon tree,
   Blue looked at the 'possum, 'possum looked at me. *Refrain*

4. Blue grinned at me, I grinned at him,
   I shook out the 'possum, Blue took him in. *Refrain*

5. Baked that 'possum all good and brown,
   And I laid them sweet potatoes 'round and 'round. *Refrain*

6. Well, old Blue died, and he died so hard,
   That he shook the ground in my back yard. *Refrain*

7. I dug his grave with a silver spade,
   I let him down with a golden chain. *Refrain*

8. When I get to heaven, first thing I'll do,
   Grab me a horn and blow for old Blue. *Refrain*

- Look at verses 6 and 7. What has happened to Old Blue? (He died and then I dug his grave.)
- On those two verses we will change the melody.

Teach verse 6 using this melody.

OLD BLUE   (Minor Version)

- Does this change the feeling of the music? (Yes) If we sang the song slowly, would that be appropriate to the words? (Yes)

Sing verse 6 of the song using the changed melody, and much slower.

- What should we do on the refrain? (Keep it the same as it was before.)

Sing verse 6 and the refrain this new way.

- We've changed the sound of the melody simply by changing one pitch and singing slower. Since we changed that one pitch, though, the melody doesn't sound as though it uses the pitches of a major scale. Does anyone know the name of another kind of scale?

Some students may know the term *minor*. This is another instance where labeling helps students recall facts. Put resonator bells on a table or desk in the order of the F-major scale.

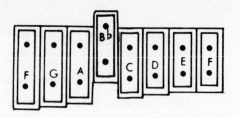

Have several students take turns playing the scale upward and downward.

• Does this sound somewhat like the accompaniment to "She'll Be Comin' Round the Mountain"? (Yes) What kind of scale is it? (Major)

Now substitute $A^\flat$ for A and $D^\flat$ for D.

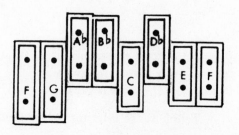

Choose a student to play this new scale. It is a harmonic minor scale. Help the students to hear the difference between the two scales and to sing them.

• Other songs can be changed from major to minor. Let's sing "Are You Sleeping?" It's in a major key.

ARE YOU SLEEPING?
Version 1: Major

FOLK ROUND FROM FRANCE

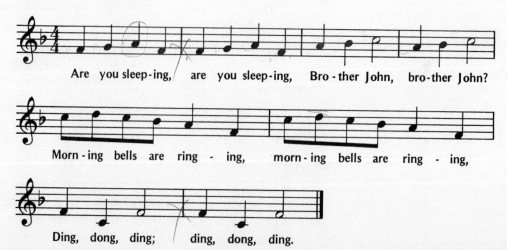

Are you sleep-ing, are you sleep-ing, Bro-ther John, bro-ther John?

Morn-ing bells are ring - ing, morn-ing bells are ring - ing,

Ding, dong, ding; ding, dong, ding.

- Now let's sing the same song in a minor key.

ARE YOU SLEEPING?
Version 2: Minor
FOLK ROUND FROM FRANCE

Are you sleep-ing, are you sleep-ing, Bro-ther John, bro-ther John?

Morn-ing bells are ring-ing, morn-ing bells are ring-ing,

Ding, dong, ding; ding, dong, ding.

ANOTHER DAY

- Here is a song that uses the pitches of a minor scale.

Play the recording of "Wade in the Water."

WADE IN THE WATER
BLACK SPIRITUAL

Wade ___ in the wa - ter, wade in the wa - ter, chil - dren,

Wade ___ in the wa - ter, God's a - gon - na trou - ble the wa - ter.

1. If Jor - dan's wa - ter is chil - ly and cold, ___ God's a-gon-na trou-ble the
2. If you ___ get there ___ be - fore ___ I do, ___

wa - ter. It chills ___ the bod - y but not ___ the soul, ___
Tell all ___ my friends ___ I'm com - in', too, ___

God's a - gon - na trou - ble the wa - ter.

- Let's sing along with the recording.
- Now, let's sing just the beginning of the song, where you sing the words "Wade in the water" the first time.
- I told you this song was in minor. Let's check to see whether I was correct. I will give you the starting pitch of the song and you sing the first three pitches of the minor scale.

After the students have sung the first three pitches of the minor scale several times, have them sing just the first and third pitches. These are the beginning pitches of "Wade in the Water." Their sound should help students identify the minor mode of the song.

- Now do you think this song really is in a minor key? (Students should be more certain by now.)
- There is a way to double-check this. Let's sing the first three pitches of the *major* scale starting with the same pitch as before. (Class sings D, E, F# several times, then D, F# several times.)
- Now, let's sing the first phrase of "Wade in the Water" using these pitches.

The students may need to try both versions several times before coming to some agreement that the first version is more like the song.

- Let's sing the whole song with the recording.

Singing with the recording is most helpful when students are learning a new song. When they are familiar with a song, give them practice in singing without accompaniment.

At another time, review this song. Students can play an Autoharp accompaniment for "Wade in the Water" using three chords: D minor (Dm), G minor (Gm), and A$_7$. On the Autoharp, the buttons for these chords are adjacent to each other and fall easily under the index, middle, and ring fingers of the left hand.

Start practice for accompanying "Wade in the Water" by having students place the left index finger on the D-minor button, cross the right arm over the left, press the button, and strum the long strings with the right hand. Once students have the coordination necessary to press the button and strum the strings at the same time, have them find the two other buttons, A$_7$ (middle finger) and G minor (ring finger), and practice changing chords between strums.[2]

The material in Strategy 9 covers several class sessions. It is not necessary to use the components of the strategy in successive class meetings. If too long a time passes between components, however, you should be prepared for a longer review time on the previous material than would ordinarily be

---

[2]See Hints for Teaching Autoharp, p. 192.

necessary. These experiences are also planned around the idea of an "unfolding" of information. The strategy begins with the use of the major scale as part of another activity, that is, as a bell part for a song. At this point, the labeling, or naming, of the scale is less important than having students *hear* the scale as an entity. The bell part is a means of reviewing the sound of a scale. The purpose of the entire strategy is to help students hear the major tonality, then begin to differentiate between major and minor tonalities. Precise reasons for the differences between major and minor scales (the half- and whole-step relationships) can wait for another strategy dealing specifically with that. Like previous strategies, this one shows inductive teaching, that is, it goes from specific instances of a concept to generalizations about that concept. In addition, this strategy shows how you can begin to help students use labels (musical terms) as part of the learning process.

STRATEGY 10 In this strategy, several kinds of learning are encouraged: defining terms such as *harmony* and *texture*, categorizing polyphonic and homophonic textures, and discriminating between textures. As children mature and the quantity and quality of their musical perceptions improve, you can develop strategies that deal with several concepts at one time.

1. Harmony occurs when two or more pitches are sounded simultaneously.
2. Texture is the relationship between melody and harmony.
3. Monophonic texture is melody without harmony.
4. In homophonic texture the melody is predominant and harmony supports it.
5. In polyphonic texture several melodies interweave, creating harmony.

Teach "New River Train" by rote.

NEW RIVER TRAIN AMERICAN FOLK SONG

I'm rid-in' that New Riv-er train,___

I'm rid-in' that New Riv-er train,___

The same old train that__ brought me here

gon-na take me back home a-gain.___

Since this part of the strategy deals with monophonic texture, it is wiser either to use your voice or to play the melody line alone on the piano when you are teaching the song.

- You've learned the song very well. Was everyone singing the same tune? (Yes)
- There is a name for music in which everyone sings the same melody at the same time. It's called monophonic. Here's a drawing that will help you remember what monophonic texture means.

Put this drawing on the chalkboard. This is a representation of monophonic texture and, with the other symbols used later in the strategy, will help students recall what they learn.

- Let's experiment. You sing your song ("New River Train") and I'll play (or sing) another song. It's one you know, so while you sing your song, keep your ears open and try to identify the song I'm playing (singing).

Sing or play "Mama Don't 'Low." Notice that "New River Train" has an eighth-note upbeat.[3]

MAMA DON'T 'LOW   AMERICAN FOLK SONG

---

[3] "Mama Don't 'Low" begins on a downbeat, or the first beat of a measure. "New River Train" begins with one eighth note that is sung before the downbeat. When the two songs are performed together, the first note of "Mama Don't 'Low" should coincide with the first syllable of "riding" in "New River Train."

- What song did I play? ("Mama Don't 'Low")
- I think you are ready to try the two songs together. Let's practice "Mama Don't 'Low" several times.
- Now, let's see if we remember "New River Train."

Divide the class into two groups. Assign one group to each song. It is easier to sing two songs together if one group starts and sings through a song one time; on the second time through, add the other song.

- Does anyone know a word for the sound we made when we sang two melodies together? (Some students may know the term *harmony*.)
- That's right. We are singing in harmony with each other. We are not singing the same pitches at the same time. Now, let's switch parts and sing our tunes in harmony once more.
- This kind of harmony is called polyphonic texture. *Poly* means "many" and *phonic* means "sound." There are many sounds going on at the same time in polyphonic texture. Here's a symbol for this kind of texture.

Put the symbol for polyphonic texture on the chalkboard.

- In polyphonic texture, there are at least two melodies of equal importance heard together.

ANOTHER DAY

Choose a student in advance to practice the Autoharp accompaniment for "Mama Don't 'Low." (See the chord symbols above the song.) This song uses G-major, D_7, and C-major chords. Have the student put the index finger on G major, the middle finger on D_7, and the ring finger on C major. Have the student strum on the first beat of each measure.

- The other day we sang two melodies together. There is a name for musical texture that has two or more equally important melodies. What is it? (Polyphonic texture)
- Today we're going to experiment with another texture. Joel is going to play for you an Autoharp part he has practiced. Can you tell what song this Autoharp part goes with? (Probably not, since this chord progression could accompany any number of songs and no melody is heard)

Have the student play the accompaniment on the Autoharp.

- Why is it so difficult to tell what song this accompaniment belongs with? (The chords give no clue as to what the melody is.)
- Let's try "Mama Don't 'Low" with Joel's accompaniment.

Have students sing with the Autoharp accompaniment.

- Did you hear harmony when you were singing? (Yes) Was it the same kind of harmony you heard when we sang "New River Train" with "Mama Don't 'Low"? (No) Why not? (The Autoharp part was made up of chords, adding harmony to the melody.) When Joel played the chords alone, there was no melody. Was it as interesting to hear just chords? (It might be at first, but it would become less interesting because there was no melody.)

- Listen to this recording. Tell me whether the harmonizing is more like putting melodies together, or like the chord accompaniment played on the Autoharp.

SHOEFLIES

WORDS AND MUSIC BY BOB SAKAYAMA

Shoe-flies fast-er than me, ___ I got-ta run, run, run, ___ or

I won't see it. And when the man says, "Fit my foot,"___

Shoe-flies.___ Dom-i-noes___

more than I do, ___ and there's a chance that he may real-ly ev-en

know more than you, ___ And when the man says,

"I don't know what to do," Dom-i-noes. ___

But-ter-flies ___ ov-er the hill, ___

You can't find ___ it then no-bod-y will. ___

And when the man says, "Bake my bread,"___ But-ter-flies. ___

- What do you think? Was the singer's melody the part you heard most? (Yes) Then is this song more like the two songs put together, polyphonic texture, or is it more like the song with the Autoharp? (It is more like the song sung with the Autoharp.) It has melody, and it has chords. This drawing will help you remember the sound of melody with harmony.

Put the symbol for melody with harmony on the chalkboard.

- When there is an obvious melody with a harmonic accompaniment that is mostly in the background, we call that sound homophonic texture.

ANOTHER DAY

Teach this song by rote.

HAVA NASHIRA   ROUND FROM ISRAEL

After the students have learned the song, have them sing it with the recording.

- We're going to try something different this time. I'll start the recording. After the singers on the recording sing the first "alleluia," you begin the song. Will you end at the same time the recording ends? (No) Why not? (The singers on the recording start before we do, so they will end before we do.)

Have students sing their part while the recording is played.

- Does anyone know what we call this kind of song? (It is a round. If necessary, give a clue such as "It's like 'Row, Row, Row Your Boat'.")
- I think we know the song well enough to try singing it as a round without the recording.

Divide the class into two groups and have them sing "Hava Nashira" as a round.

- Think about how texture works in a round. Is it more like adding chords, or like singing two songs together? Is it more like homophonic texture or polyphonic texture?

After discussion the class should realize that although in a round everyone sings the same melody, there is harmony because groups of singers start at different times. All the parts in a round are equally important, so a round has polyphonic texture.

- A round is special because it has imitation. The second group sings the same melody as the first, or *imitates* it. Here's a diagram to show this kind of texture.

ANOTHER DAY

- Let's see whether you can hear the difference between monophonic, homophonic, and polyphonic textures.

Put these drawings on the chalkboard.

Monophonic   Homophonic   Polyphonic

- As I play each piece of recorded music, decide which drawing best fits what you hear. Remember, if you hear a melody alone, what is the texture called? (Monophonic) What term is used to describe a melody with chord accompaniment? (Homophonic) Tell what polyphonic means. (Two or more melodies of equal importance heard together)

The questions are not all asked in the same way. In the first two questions students are asked to describe by labeling; in the last question the label is given and the students are asked to define it.

Play the recording of *What Do You Hear? Texture* (record 1).

After the students have listened and made their responses, play the recording again. Stop after each selection to discuss which answer is correct and why. Correct answers are shown in color.

WHAT DO YOU HEAR? TEXTURE

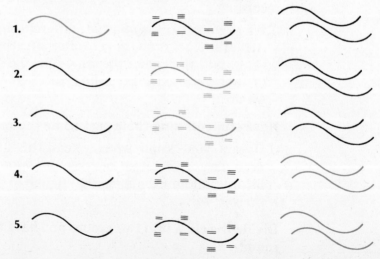

1.

2.

3.

4.

5.

STRATEGY 11 One of your goals as a teacher is to help students become increasingly independent. This strategy has three activities intended to develop independence in recognizing sections in musical form.

> A piece of music may have sections, distinguishable through unity and contrast.

- Let's review a song we've heard before.

DRY BONES BLACK SPIRITUAL

Ⓐ
E - ze - kiel cried, "Them dry bones!" E - ze - kiel cried, "Them dry bones!"
E - ze - kiel cried, "Them dry bones!" Now hear the word of the Lord.

Ⓑ
gradually getting faster
The foot bone con - nect - ed to the leg bone,
The leg bone con - nect - ed to the knee bone,
The knee bone con - nect - ed to the hip bone,
The hip bone con - nect - ed to the back bone,
The back bone con - nect - ed to the shoul - der bone,
The shoul - der bone con - nect - ed to the neck bone,
The neck bone con - nect - ed to the jaw bone,

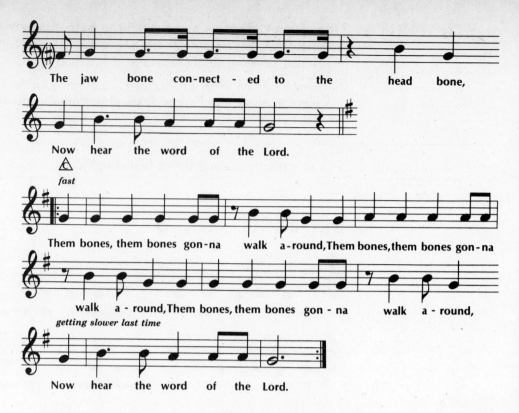

The jaw bone con-nect-ed to the head bone,

Now hear the word of the Lord.

fast

Them bones, them bones gon-na walk a-round, Them bones, them bones gon-na

walk a-round, Them bones, them bones gon-na walk a-round,

getting slower last time

Now hear the word of the Lord.

- This time, when you sing "Dry Bones," think about how many bones are being connected to each other.

Use visual cues, such as pointing to parts of the body, to help the class discover what nine bones are connected: foot, leg, knee, hip, back, shoulder, neck, jaw, and head.

- Good. You found all the bones. Is anything else happening in the song? (Yes. One part says "Ezekiel cried.")
- How many different sections are there? (Three)
- Let's look at the second section. There is a rest, or a silence, before you sing the name of the bone that the foot bone is connected to. What is the name of that bone? (Leg)
- Where we hear a silence in the melody, let's play a sound. What instrument could we use? (A tone block, wood block, or some other wooden sound would be appropriate.)
- Jenny, choose an instrument that reminds you of the leg bone.

Continue with instruments such as

Knee	Small drum
Hip	Large cymbals
Back	Xylophone
Shoulder	Finger cymbals
Neck	Guiro (scraped)
Jaw	Triangle
Head	Large drum

In this strategy, students are asked to do several kinds of thinking: describing, labeling, categorizing, and discriminating. They are also asked to recognize symbols. Each successive step in the strategy depends in some way on perceptions and conceptualizations that took place in previous steps. Learning proceeds from the specific to the general.

- Remember to play your instrument only on the rest. Let's practice the second section only. Those of you without instruments help us by chanting the words in rhythm.

Students may have to practice this several times. Help at first by pointing to the players when it is their turn to play.

- That was very good. Let's sing that section with the instrumental accompaniment.
- What else could our instruments do in this song? (All could play on the third section to show how the bones are walking around.)
- Excellent. How about the first section? Is it different from the last section? (Yes. Ezekiel is doing some announcing.)
- What could be done there? (Someone could sing a solo.)

There are other solutions to varying the first and last sections. Have the class perform "Dry Bones" with all the changes and additions to emphasize the form.

ANOTHER DAY

- The other day we found that "Dry Bones" has three sections. Today we're going to try something new with another song.

In the following activity, a small learning task is identified, then extended until a whole sequence of learning tasks has been completed.

- You remember the hand motions we did with a song. When you put together a whole set of motions, they are called a "hand jive."

Practice the following hand jive with the class.
   Pat knees four times
   Clap hands four times
   Palms down, pass the right hand across above the left four times
   Palms down, pass the left hand across above the right four times
   Touch left elbow with right palm four times (left index finger points upward)
   Touch right elbow with left palm four times (right index finger points upward)
   "Thumb a ride" over the left shoulder four times
   "Thumb a ride" over the right shoulder four times

- Good. Now, every time you see this sign on the chalkboard, go all the way through the hand jive.

- Now listen to the recording. It's easy to feel the beat in this song.

Play the recording of "Shoeflies" (record 1), stopping after the first vocal section.

- When the music starts, feel the beat silently. Count eight beats without making a sound.

Play the beginning of the recording so students can become familiar with the music and practice counting the first eight beats silently.

- Let's use eight marks as a reminder to count the first eight beats silently.

Put eight beat marks (two measures) on the chalkboard.

- Be ready to snap your fingers on the beat. Snap once for every *X* with a stem on it.

Add four measures of *X*'s with stems to the signs that are already on the chalkboard. Practice with the class.

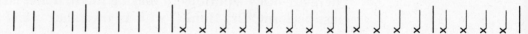

- The hand jive comes next. Each time you hear a man singing, we'll be doing the hand jive.

Add this sign to the others and practice up to this point with the recording.

- Good. Look at the signs that stand for motions you can do with the whole song.

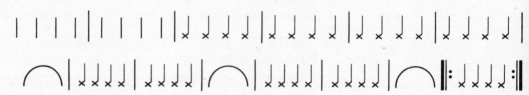

- There are repeat marks in the last measure. Keep snapping your fingers as you hear the music get softer and fade away.

Practice for this activity could well extend to several class periods and be interspersed with other activities.

ANOTHER DAY

Put the entire diagram on the chalkboard again.

- These signs show more than the motions to the song. Listen to the recording again. Follow the signs on the chalkboard to see how they show what you hear in the music.

The curved lines coincide with the vocal sections. Beat marks and *X*'s coincide with the instrumental parts: Introduction, Interludes, and Coda.

ANOTHER DAY

- Let's listen to this composition. You will hear two different melodies in it.

- In addition to the two melodies, you can hear a man's voice calling numbers. This time listen through four call numbers.
- Let's see how good you are at discovering when the melodies change.

Put this chart on the chalkboard:

1. Introduction
2. Melody A
3. Melody A   Melody B
4. Melody A   Melody B
5. Melody A   Melody B
6. Interlude
7. Melody A   Melody B
8. Melody A   Melody B
9. Melody A   Melody B
10. Melody A   Melody B
11. Coda

- At which numbers will you have to choose between Melody A and Melody B? (Numbers 3, 4, 5, 7, 8, 9 and 10)

Play the recording and have students write on a piece of paper which melody they hear at each call number. Review the answers: Introduction, AABA, Interlude, AABA, Coda.

Play the recording again and help students determine which melody they hear in each section. If there is some confusion, draw a visual representation using dots or lines (or both) to show the first few notes of each melody.

GENERALIZATIONS

The following generalizations may be drawn from the discussion.

Inherent Musical Qualities
All music has inherent stylistic qualities. Some of these qualities are melody, rhythm, form, tone color, texture, and dynamics.

Sensitivity
Children develop musical sensitivity by becoming aware of these qualities in music and by becoming more knowledgeable about them.

Materials
Materials are chosen to accommodate a range of abilities within one age level and between different age groups.

Activities
Activities are selected to provide for a range of abilities and preferences.

ASSESSMENT 1

STRATEGY 12
Study the three activities that follow. They involve singing (with Autoharp accompaniment), moving, and listening. They are arranged in a learning sequence. Indicate (a) what inherent musical quality can be emphasized, (b) what concepts you think are being presented, and (c) how you would teach each activity.

---

[4]Adapted from Call Chart 9: Form, in *Silver Burdett Music 6* (Morristown, N.J.: Silver Burdett Company, 1981), p. 145.

ACTIVITY 1

Use Autoharp accompaniment.

STREETS OF LAREDO AMERICAN COWBOY SONG

1. As I _____ walked out in the streets of La - re - do,
2. "I see by your out - fit that you are a cow - boy,"

As I walked out in La - re - do one day,
These words he said as I bold - ly walked by;

I spied a young cow - boy wrapped up in white lin - en,
"Come lis - ten to me and I'll tell my sad sto - ry.

Wrapped up in white lin - en and cold as the clay.
I'm shot in the chest and I'm sure I will die.

3. "Now once in the saddle I used to ride handsome,
   'A handsome young cowboy' is what they would say.
   I'd ride into town and go down to the card-house,
   But I'm shot in the chest and I'm dying today.

4. "Go run to the spring for a cup of cold water
   To cool down my fever," the young cowboy said.
   But when I returned, his poor soul had departed,
   And I wept when I saw the young cowboy was dead.

5. We'll bang the drum slowly and play the fife lowly,
   We'll play the dead march as we bear him along.
   We'll go to the graveyard and lay the sod o'er him;
   He was a young cowboy, but he had done wrong.

ACTIVITY 2

Practice the waltz step, a pattern of threes. On beat one of each measure, take a somewhat long step and bend the knee slightly. On beats two and three, take shorter steps. Think "down, up, up, down, up, up" or "1, 2, 3, 1, 2, 3." Take one step for each beat: Left, right, left; Right, left, right.

　　Use the recording.

◉ German Dance

Stand in a large circle facing the center. Do waltz steps as follows:

4 measures forward
4 measures backward
2 measures, moving the circle to the left
2 measures, moving the circle to the right
2 measures turning to the left in a small circle, alone
2 measures turning to the right in a small circle, alone

Repeat all the steps, facing the center of the circle as the music ends.

ACTIVITY 3

Brahms: Sonata in E Flat Major for Clarinet
and Piano, Opus 20, No. 2, II

ASSESSMENT 2 Write a strategy using several activities to teach the following concept to nine-, ten-, and eleven-year-olds.

> Melodies can be extended by the use of many kinds of compositional devices. Two compositional devices are repetition and contrast.

Include in your strategy (a) suggested dialogue with the class, (b) directions you would give the class, (c) what you are having the class do at a given time, and (d) music you would use.

4 *Planning Instruction*

Write a lesson plan. Show how the lesson relates to long- and short-range plans. Specify

(a) students' level of achievement when instruction begins,

(b) musical objectives,

(c) activities and materials to be used, and

(d) ways of measuring achievement.

Most successful learning experiences begin with a well thought-out plan. It is a rare teacher who can stand before a class and extemporize with any degree of success. Even with a plan, there is no guarantee that all lessons will meet with enthusiastic response. However, success is more likely to be achieved if plans are carefully formulated, keeping the following considerations in mind:

1. Who are my students?
2. What shall I teach them?
3. Why should I teach it?
4. How shall I teach it?
5. How much time do I have?
6. What results do I expect and how shall I measure them?
7. Should my students help me plan?
8. What kinds of plans will guide my teaching?

WHO ARE MY STUDENTS?

To plan effectively, you will need information about each student. Learn about developmental levels, reading levels, behavior problems, and handicapping conditions. Check office records; consult with guidance counselors and last year's teachers; talk with special education teachers if handicapped children are to be mainstreamed.

Knowing the developmental levels of students can be crucial to planning. Children must pay attention in order to learn, and their attention span is short. Some teachers use the rule of thumb that children's attention span in minutes equals their age in years: a child of six years has an attention span of six minutes. Others think that the attention span of nearly anyone is seven minutes plus or minus one or two. In any case the attention span of individuals in a group must be considered in planning.

You should consider the language problems of individual students. Some may have difficulty in reading aloud. They should not be embarrassed by being called on to "read the words of the first verse to the class." Some children may have difficulty expressing themselves verbally. They should not be asked to explain what happens to the melody at the end of "Brother Noah," but rather to show the direction of the ending by moving or by playing it on resonator bells.

You need to be aware of the social development of the students. If students, no matter what their chronological age, are not yet mature enough to work together without continual conflict, the teacher cannot plan activities that require them to work in small groups, where cooperation is essential. If there are behavior problems, plans should call for very structured and well-defined responses.

Some mainstreamed students may have different styles of learning and may need visual, auditory, or tactile and kinesthetic stimulation. Others may have different rates of learning and may need more time to accomplish tasks.

You should consider the academic level of the students so that books and other materials are not too easy and boring, or too hard and discouraging; so that words used in questions and directions are within their vocabularies and therefore understood; so that learning activities are rooted in a background of pertinent experiences.

Most important, however, you must realize that students are children and that children are better able to comprehend what is taught by activities than what is taught by words. Good planning requires provision for activities rather than talk, for participation in the musical experience — singing, playing instruments, moving, creating.

Study the following lesson plan. Be prepared to specify (1) the age of the group, (2) the reading level, (3) any behavior problem, and (4) whether there are handicapped children in the group.

Materials	Music book Record player Rhythm instruments, bells Pictures Word strips Recording
Objective	Demonstrate ability to differentiate between loud and soft through singing, through movement, and through selection of rhythm instruments.
Entry Behavior	Students have had one lesson on differentiating loud and soft, with 70 percent of the students responding appropriately. Academic achievement is at grade level. Two mainstreamed children are from the Learning Disabled Group.

Procedure Show the pictures of the sleeping baby and the jackhammer on the street to remind students of the two ways they sang "I'm Gonna Sing" (page 9) in their last lesson.

Review the song, singing it both loudly and softly. Work on the words as needed.

Review playing the bells on the first beat of each measure, giving students who have not played a turn. Have the class evaluate the playing.

Have students play follow-the-leader and walk to the steady beat as they listen to "Zion's Children."

ZION'S CHILDREN BLACK SPIRITUAL

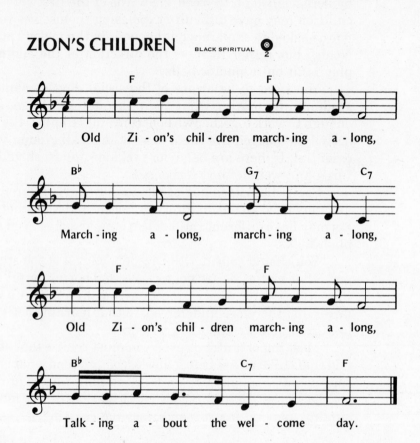

Old Zi-on's chil-dren march-ing a-long,

March-ing a-long, march-ing a-long,

Old Zi-on's chil-dren march-ing a-long,

Talk-ing a-bout the wel-come day.

Practice starting and stopping to a drumbeat only, if necessary.

Change the word *marching* to *tiptoe* and ask students to identify the picture that matches tiptoeing.

Sing the song, having the students tiptoe. Ask if their feet will sound soft or loud.

Ask students how they would play the drum to match the sound of tiptoeing. (Lightly or perhaps on the rim)

Ask students to choose a different instrument to play on the tiptoe part. (Triangle or finger cymbals)

Teach children to sing "Zion's Children." Emphasize either soft or loud singing, depending on the words used.

Test students' ability to recall a melody by humming "All Night, All Day" (page 11). See if students remember the name of the song.

Ask if the song was sung loudly or softly.

Sing "All Night, All Day" with the class. Work on words as necessary.

Have students choose and play a suitable instrument with "All Night, All Day."

Use pictures to remind students how they showed loud and soft by their singing, tiptoeing, and choosing and playing instruments.

Label the pictures with word strips:

| Loud | Soft |

Ask children to think of other ways to move that would be soft (bend, stretch) or loud (jump), so that in the next music lesson they can move in those ways.

After studying the plan just outlined, you should conclude the following:

1. The lesson is intended for six-year-olds because
   - books are not required
   - physical activity is included
   - songs have a limited range
   - songs use a limited vocabulary.

2. The lesson takes into consideration children with behavior problems by including
   - short and varied activities to take care of short attention span
   - physical activity to relieve tensions.

3. The lesson takes into consideration children with learning disabilities by using
   - pictures for visual learners
   - movement for those who have a special need for kinesthetic and tactile learning experiences.

WHAT SHALL I TEACH THEM?

Since the entire first section of this book is devoted to what to teach, a few reminders should suffice here. First, in planning lessons, choose materials of good quality that appeal to you and that you can present with enthusiasm. In many instances, music that lends itself to learning about more than one element will be appealing both to you and to your students. For example, the teaching procedure suggested for "Hand Me Down" (page 19) focused on upward and downward melodic direction. The song could also exemplify ABA form, *D.C. al Fine*, call and response, different kinds of cadences, and melodic fragments that stay on one pitch. These learnings are obvious and uncomplicated; they can be taught through singing, playing instruments, improvising accompaniments, movement, and visual aids. All these activities are suitable for the age and developmental level of elementary school children. On the other hand, the music you find most appealing is often too subtle or too complex for your students.

In Beethoven's Fifth Symphony, for example, there are many musical learnings you can focus on, but your students cannot comprehend so complex a structure as the form of its first movement. If, however, you are just as enthusiastic over the form of "Get on Board" (page 12), a straightforward, uncomplicated example of ABA form, with a great deal of appeal for six-year-olds, your own enthusiasm will be contagious and the lesson will end with the children looking forward to their next music class.

Second, you should choose materials that provide for growth in musical perception and skill development. You should be certain to include songs that can be accompanied with the Autoharp; that have phrases or entire sections that can be played on resonator bells; that can inspire a planned or an improvised accompaniment on percussion instruments; that have countermelodies; and that increase sensitivity to vocal quality, phrasing, diction, and shading.

Finally, you should choose materials that relate to what has been taught in previous lessons and to what you will teach in the future. A series of isolated, one-session learning experiences that have no relation to one another cannot possibly provide the growth and development that will result from a series of well-planned, related lessons that have clearly started somewhere and are logically progressing toward a predetermined goal.

WHY SHOULD I TEACH IT?

Before you can effectively plan even a single lesson, you must be convinced of the importance of music in the total curriculum. If you regard music as an unimportant subject, this will be reflected not only in your planning but also in your teaching. Children are very perceptive; they are quick to "read" teachers' attitudes, and they can tell when a teacher is insincere.

When you plan your lessons, it is your responsibility to decide which songs, listening selections, and activities you will include; it is also your responsibility to justify your choice — if only to yourself. You must continually ask yourself, "Is this a valid musical experience? Will this activity really help reinforce what the children learned last week?" This does not mean that every single song or activity the teacher includes in a lesson has to reflect concepts that were introduced in the last class period. It simply means that the main portion of the lesson will focus on concepts.

A wise teacher also has a contingency plan ready to be used at any time. A contingency plan may mean scrapping the plan altogether, changing the order of the procedure, or changing the pace by omitting or adding activities or materials. No matter how valid the musical experience you have planned, if the students are not "with you," nothing will be gained.

Here is a plan for the song "Old Blue." It is intended for a group of third-grade students. This class is usually very well behaved; they seem to enjoy movement activities and are able to function when given quite a lot of freedom. Consider a situation, however, in which the regular teacher is absent, there was a fight on the playground, and students have just returned from a fire drill. How would you modify the plan under these circumstances?

Materials "Old Blue" (page 36, record 1)
Music book
Autoharp
Overhead projector
Box of rhythm instruments

Concept   Music has long and short sounds.

Objectives
1. Sing the new song accurately, with special attention to sustaining long tones at the ends of phrases.
2. Improvise with rhythm instruments, using both long and short sounds.
3. Play, sing, identify, and label tied notes.

Procedure   Have students find a space in the room where they can move their arms and torsos, remaining in one place.

Ask students to move until the sound of the Autoharp stops and then "freeze."

Strum the chords of "Old Blue" as follows. (Stop the sound by placing the hand over the strings to stop vibration.)

```
F | F . . . (stop)
F | C₇ . . . (stop)
C₇ | C₇ | C₇ | F
F | C₇ . . . (stop)
C₇ | F . . . (stop), etc.
```

Praise students who move in different ways in relation to the sounds of the Autoharp, reflecting long and short sounds, high and low sounds, loud and soft sounds.

Have students sit down. Repeat the song at least three times and have students listen selectively, as follows.

1. Have them observe as you draw a long mark on the chalkboard for each of the long tones they hear (first listening).

> I had an old dog_____
> And his name was Blue_____
> etc.

2. Have them identify the words that occur on each of the long tones (second listening).
3. Have them use hand motions to show the length of each long tone (third listening).

Ask students to use their books to find the places where the long tones occur. Then ask them to sing only those words, as they listen to the rest of the song.

Have students sing the whole song.

Ask students to think of a way to make a long sound with their hands or feet (such as rubbing palms together or rubbing feet on the floor), then think of a way to make a short sound with their hands or feet (such as clapping, snapping, stamping).

Have students choose instruments that can sustain the long sounds (e.g., tambourine, maracas, sand blocks) and other instruments that cannot (e.g., wood block, claves).

Have students walk on short sounds and stretch or bend on long sounds.

Sing the song again, reminding students to hold the long sounds for their full value. Draw students' attention to the notation over the words that are held. Review the durations of whole notes and quarter notes. Point out the line that ties them together and identify it as a tie. Explain that the tie indicates that the two tones are to be tied together or held for the value of both.

How would you modify the plan? There are probably as many ways as there are music teachers. Here are some suggestions for changing the plan to get and keep the attention of an unsettled class.

1. Change the order of procedure. A class that is upset may not be able to handle the freedom of being out of their seats, especially at the beginning of the period. To begin the lesson, an activity requiring a more structured response should be chosen. Examples include echo clapping, singing a familiar or a favorite song, or completing a short paper-and-pencil exercise such as the following.

Draw a line under the correct word in each group.

UPWARD
<u>DOWNWARD</u>
SAME

UPWARD
DOWNWARD
<u>SAME</u>

STEPS
<u>LEAPS</u>

STEPS
<u>LEAPS</u>

2. Change the focus. If you have planned a one-concept lesson, stay with the concept only as long as students are attentive. Then introduce favorite material that can be performed well, so that you can be generous in your praise.
3. Change the entire plan. Introduce music the students thoroughly enjoy, including their favorite songs and some popular music.

Unless the class is orderly and attentive to the lesson, it will not matter what you teach, and no one will benefit. While the main goal is to help students discover how music works, you must never forget to provide opportunities for children to experience music for the sheer joy of it.

HOW SHALL I TEACH IT?

Two ways of teaching a single concept are presented in Chapter 5, "Using Deductive and Inductive Approaches." However, there is no one right way to teach any lesson. The right way is the way that works. Each classroom situation is unique; students have different needs, are at different levels of development, and have different response modes. (The plans of successful teachers usually include appeals to the senses — sight, sound, and touch.) Consider all available information about each student and then try to reach each one. Be flexible enough to discard approaches that do not work, and be concerned enough to experiment until the right ones are found.

No matter what approaches you finally adopt, you must always keep one thing in mind — you cannot expect your students to run before they can walk. You cannot expect your students to play "Twinkle, Twinkle, Little Star" in tune on the recorder until they can play a single tone in tune. You cannot expect your students to sing "Beside the Sea" in harmony until they can sing the melody in unison. You cannot expect your students to perceive two rhythm patterns that occur simultaneously until they can perceive one rhythm pattern by itself. You cannot expect your students to categorize musical events until they can recognize and define them.

It is important, therefore, that as you plan, you establish a realistic order for the goals and objectives that you expect your students to reach, beginning with simple things and gradually progressing to the complex. Remember to plan for small steps in perception, skill development, and cognition. As you select music for your classes, keep in mind the concepts to be taught. Begin with music in which the elements or qualities you are teaching are in the foreground and easily identified, and in which parts to be sung and played are easy. Progress in small steps to music that is more subtle and complex.

HOW MUCH TIME DO I HAVE?

The length and the frequency of music periods are important considerations in your planning. If you have class periods of forty-five minutes, you will be able to plan and teach in more depth than if you have only twenty-minute periods. Similarly, if your class meets three times a week for a year, you can plan to accomplish more and teach in greater detail than if your class meets only once a week.

Some schools use modular, or cyclical, scheduling, in which one group of children has a music class every day for a period of six to ten weeks. At the end of that time, the group may go on to daily art lessons for the next six- to ten-week period, while another group has music, and so forth. This type of scheduling gives teachers a unique opportunity, for it enables them to divide the six- to ten-week period into units of specific concentration. For example, the chief focus of the first two weeks might be on learning to play the recorder, and another two weeks could be on singing in harmony. Some teachers may prefer to spend the entire time concentrating on one activity. If one activity such as recorder playing is taught, care must be taken that recorder playing is not the *only* activity provided in the music classes during that time. Although a portion of each lesson may be devoted to it, provision for other activities should be made so that those students who have difficulty playing recorder, or just don't enjoy playing it, will experience success or enjoyment in another part of the lesson.

If a teacher is responsible for planning assembly programs that include music, the length of time students will have for preparation is crucial. It will determine how much music can be included and how difficult that music can be.

Some teachers approach realistic planning by counting exactly the number of class periods each group will have during the semester or the year, excluding days that school is not in session. If a class meets once a week, they will have about thirty periods of music instruction during the school year. That is not very much time, and the teacher must be able to give an honest answer to this question: In precisely which ways have students benefited as a result of those thirty (or sixty, or eighty) class periods?

Teachers have to learn to deal with another aspect of time: how to lengthen or shorten a planned lesson. Sometimes a skill that seemed easily within the grasp of the class eludes them and takes much longer than was anticipated. Sometimes everything that was planned is accomplished in half a period. A class period can be extended for unexpected reasons beyond your control (the classroom teacher is in conference and cannot take the class); or the class period can be shortened (bad weather can cause school to open late).

Consider the following plan and think about how you would modify it to make it shorter or longer.

Materials   Music books
Rhythm instruments
Resonator bells (two sets)

Concept   Music can have monophonic, homophonic, or polyphonic texture.

Objectives   1. Perform "Toembaï" in three ways, demonstrating monophonic, homophonic, and polyphonic textures.
2. Label monophonic, homophonic, and polyphonic textures and describe their differences.

Entry Behavior   Students have learned to sing "Toembaï" and have had many experiences with monophonic, homophonic, and polyphonic textures. This is a mature fifth-grade class.

Procedure   Clap the rhythm of "Toembaï" without singing it. Ask whether students recall the song; if not, sing part of it for them.

TOEMBAÏ   ROUND FROM ISRAEL

USED BY PERMISSION OF WORLD AROUND SONGS.

Toem - baï, toem - baï, toem - baï, toem - baï, toem - baï, toem - baï, toem - baï.

Tra la la   la la la la la   la la la la la   la.

Tra la la la   la   la la la la   la   la la la la la   la.

Have the class sing the song in unison, unaccompanied. Review the musical term for the texture of the music as just performed (*monophonic*).

Have the class sing the song in unison again, this time clapping the steady beat while moving the hands as follows:

1. Move hands to the right during the first phrase and back to the center on the repeat.
2. Move hands to the left on the second phrase and back to the center on the repeat.
3. Move hands upward on the third phrase and down on the repeat.

Divide the class into three groups and have them sing the song as a three-part round.

Have the class sing the song as a three-part round again, this time clapping the steady beat and using the hand movements as above. Review the term for the texture of the music as just performed (*polyphonic*).

After the students are familiar with "Toembaï," divide the class into small groups for the following activities. (See further discussion in Chapter 6, "Teaching Large and Small Groups.")

SMALL GROUP 1: EIGHT STUDENTS

    a. Have students create a circle dance that fits "Toembaï."

    b. Have students practice the dance in two ways:

        (1) As an interpretation of monophonic texture (all doing the same thing at the same time)

        (2) As an interpretation of polyphonic texture (four students in each group performing the dance as a two-part round).

    c. If the group needs help, recall the clapping and hand movement procedure and suggest that students adapt that — for example, circle to the right, then back; move toward the center, then back; swing your partner with left arm, then right arm.

SMALL GROUP 2: TEN STUDENTS

    a. Have students create a bell accompaniment for "Toembaï," using two sets of resonator bells as follows:

        (1) Assign three students to play the E-minor chord (E,G,B).

        (2) Assign four students to play the B_7 chord (B,D#,F#,A).

        (3) Assign three students to play the A-minor chord (A,C,E).

    b. Have the three bell-player groups practice the chords until they can play them as an accompaniment to "Toembaï."

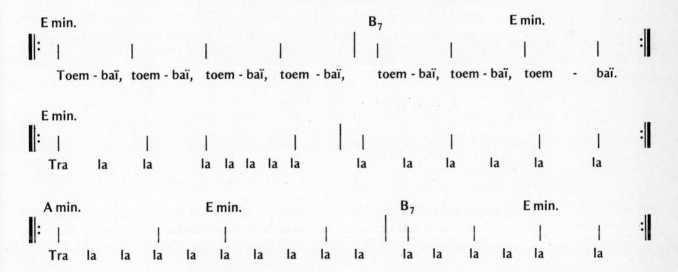

SMALL GROUP 3: TWELVE STUDENTS

    a. Have students perform "Toembaï" as follows:

        (1) In unison, without accompaniment

        (2) In two groups, each group singing on a different vowel sound (for example, *oh, ah, oo, ee*)

        (3) In two groups as a two-part round (sung twice — once using words; once using vowel sounds and rhythm instruments that each group has chosen previously)

        (4) In three groups as a three-part round (sung three times — using words, vowel sounds, and rhythm instruments).

When students in small groups 1, 2, and 3 are ready, have them perform for each other.

Have students in small groups 2 and 3 perform in the following manner (you may wish to tape record the performances):

1. Small group 2 — chords only, no melody
2. Small group 3 — melody with no accompaniment
3. Small group 3 — melody beginning at three different times (three-part round)
4. Small groups 2 and 3 — unison melody with chord accompaniment.

Play the tape and have the class label and describe the texture of each performance as harmony only, monophonic, polyphonic, or homophonic.

How could you modify the above plan to lengthen it? One possibility would be to have each group perform each assignment. Some skilled students could act as peer tutors. If everyone were given the opportunity to do each assignment, the lesson would become about three times as long. Or you could relate the song to other areas of the curriculum. For example, you could discuss the place of origin of the song (Israel) and relate the song to ethnic music of the Middle East. Think of other ways to lengthen this lesson.

How could you shorten the lesson? One suggestion might be to omit singing the song as a three-part round. Or you could leave out the hand movement/clapping exercise. Remember, do not feel compelled to finish the lesson. Unfinished and interesting tasks can provide strong motivation for the next lesson. For example, the taping or the performances for the class or both could be postponed until the next session. Think of other ways to shorten the lesson.

WHAT RESULTS DO I EXPECT AND HOW SHALL I MEASURE THEM?

In many schools teachers are given a special book in which they write plans for the year. Each page of the plan book is divided into a number of boxes, and each box is intended for a day's plan in a single subject area. Many plan books have the word *objective* printed at the top of each box, with a space for the teacher to write the goal, or intent, of the plan. The teacher might simply write

Objective   Teach AB form, or

Objective   Understand that music can be loud or soft

Surely, both objectives express the intent of the teacher, but what happens when, two days after the lesson has been taught, the six-year-old students can't find section B in a new piece of music? The teacher looks back in the plan book and says, "But I taught that! Why don't they remember it?" The fact is that even though the teacher presented the concept, the students never really learned it, and the teacher did not know that until the students tried to apply the concept to new material.

In the 1960s and 1970s when huge sums of federal money were being spent on elementary and secondary education, the Department of Health, Education, and Welfare wanted proof that students were benefiting from these monetary grants. They stipulated that to receive a grant, objectives had to be written in behavioral terms — in terms that would state (1) the content to be learned, (2) the process by which the learner showed that the learning had taken place, and (3) the minimum skill or knowledge level that was acceptable.

Rather than showing only the intent of the teacher, as the above objectives do, behavioral objectives are stated with built-in evaluations that let the teacher know immediately whether or not the students have mastered what has been taught. These are called behavioral objectives, or performance objectives, because they require the students to show by some overt action (behavior) that they have achieved a specific objective.

If the first objective were stated in behavioral terms, it would read as follows:

Objective Given a song in AB form, demonstrate the ability to hear the difference between two sections (the music content to be learned) by pointing to *A* when section A is heard and to *B* when section B is heard (the process by which the learner shows that the learning has taken place). The response will be accurate in two of three consecutive class sessions (the minimum skill or knowledge level acceptable).

Some teachers also include the projected time for mastery (the number of lessons). It may take longer and be more cumbersome to state objectives in this form, but it is much better to be able to plan future lessons on the basis of what the students have demonstrated they know than what the teacher only assumes they know. Once this mode of planning is established, stating objectives in measurable terms becomes second nature. Then they can be stated more simply. For example,

Objective Show the difference between loud and soft by clapping on the loud section and patting knees on the soft sections.

No matter what wording they use, successful teachers usually include in their planning (1) the musical content to be learned, (2) the process that will show the learning has taken place, and (3) the minimum skill or knowledge level acceptable.

Study the lesson plans in this chapter. Are objectives stated in measurable terms? Give reasons for your answers.

There are three kinds of objectives that can be helpful in your planning. Behavioral objectives state what the student must do to demonstrate mastery of the objectives. However, the teacher must also have a clear picture of what teacher and student will do together to bring about mastery. Instructional objectives, then, describe teacher and student behavior in specific learning situations and include the materials and procedures to be used. Finally, program objectives indicate what is to be achieved over a longer period of time — a semester, a year, a lifetime.

SHOULD MY STUDENTS HELP ME PLAN?

It is the teacher's responsibility to establish the long-range, or program, objectives for music classes and to formulate daily or weekly plans that progress toward those objectives. Whenever possible, students should be encouraged to participate in formulating plans for the next class period so that the class becomes "ours" rather than "yours," and so that students grow in their ability to evaluate progress. If at the end of a class period the teacher asks a simple question, such as "Do you think we have learned to recognize the difference between beats grouped in sets of two and sets of three," the way may be paved for its review at the next lesson and this may help to insure cooperation on the part of the students. It may help them begin to evaluate their own learning.

In many schools each class is called on to present an assembly program at some time during the year. This can be an ideal opportunity for teacher and students to plan together, exchange ideas, and decide what works best. The teacher can turn the planning session into a learning experience by helping students realize why some of their ideas are better than others. For instance, if students suggest that only popular music be included in their program, the teacher might help them broaden the repertoire by suggesting that the audience would enjoy knowing about the variety of music encountered in class. If the teacher includes students in the planning, they must be listened to and their suggestions must be given serious consideration. The teacher who only pays lip service to students' suggestions would do better to leave the students out of the planning altogether. If conflict arises during a planning session, the teacher must be the final authority, and this should be understood from the beginning. However, it is amazing how little conflict occurs when everyone understands that the objective for all is to plan the best possible program.

WHAT KINDS OF PLANS WILL GUIDE MY TEACHING?

There are three kinds of plans you can and should make to guide your teaching: (1) long-range plans (program objectives); (2) short-range plans (instructional objectives); and (3) lesson plans. If you have taken the time to investigate, you have a pretty good idea of what you can expect from your students, even before you meet them for the first time. Having determined where your students are academically, you must decide how much you want them to accomplish during their stay with you, whether it be a year, a semester, or ten weeks. You begin by formulating a long-range plan.

LONG-RANGE PLANS

A long-range plan is a general plan. It is usually not specific about what will be taught or the materials that will be used. It simply defines the goals that you expect your students to attain. Sometimes the responsibility for deciding what and how much should be taught is left entirely to the teacher. More often than not, however, the school system helps the teacher by providing a curriculum guide that states the goals for each level in all subjects.

The General Music Objectives (page 67) will serve as an example. They are extracted from the Anne Arundel County (Maryland) Public Schools Curriculum Guide. In this guide, the teacher is given specific suggestions for each of eight categories. Students are expected to demonstrate growth in each category by the end of the school year. (This guide is intended for fully qualified music teachers who meet their classes at least twice each week.)

GENERAL MUSIC OBJECTIVES: GRADE FOUR[1]

O – not attempted; 1 – poor; 2 – fair; 3 – good; 4 – excellent
Assessments may be used individually or in groups

1. LISTENING   *The student will demonstrate perceptive listening through*

Date   Assessment

_____   ____   **a.** movement and more complex dances
_____   ____   **b.** imitative performances
_____   ____   **c.** visual representations
_____   ____   **d.** verbal descriptions
_____   ____   **e.** traditional notation and music terminology

2. PERFORMING   *The student will demonstrate the ability to perform music through*

_____   ____   **a.** learning and singing at least twenty new songs
_____   ____   **b.** using the body as an instrument
_____   ____   **c.** manipulating environmental sound sources
_____   ____   **d.** playing the ukulele

3. READING AND WRITING   *The student will read and write*

_____   ____   **a.** traditional music symbols and notation

4. CREATING   *The student will demonstrate the ability to create music by*

_____   ____   **a.** improvising
_____   ____   **b.** arranging
_____   ____   **c.** composing

5. STRUCTURE   *The student will demonstrate understanding of the structural features of music by performing, organizing, or describing*

_____   ____   **a.** rhythm (eighth note/dotted quarter pattern, dotted quarter/eighth note pattern, six-eight meter, andante, presto)
_____   ____   **b.** melody (fa, ti, transposition/modulation/register)
_____   ____   **c.** harmony (two-part cadences; partner songs; two-part harmony; I, IV, V, and V_7 accompaniments)
_____   ____   **d.** tone color (orchestral instruments and families)
_____   ____   **e.** form (rondo)
_____   ____   **f.** symbols and terms (bass clef and note names on grand staff)

6. LITERATURE AND HISTORY   *The student will perform, organize, and describe a variety of*

_____   ____   **a.** musical styles and periods
_____   ____   **b.** ethnic music

7. RESOURCES AND EXPERIENCES   *The student will*

_____   ____   **a.** perform in musical organizations
_____   ____   **b.** use community music resources
_____   ____   **c.** attend music activities that are curriculum related

8. EVALUATING AND VALUING   *The student will demonstrate evidence of*

_____   ____   **a.** evaluating music
_____   ____   **b.** valuing music

---

[1]Courtesy of R. Bruce Horner, Coordinator of Music, Anne Arundel County Public Schools.

In some systems the curriculum guide or the course of study may become "the plan" to be followed without variation, while in others the teacher may use it only as a resource. The policy varies from system to system. The focus of this discussion will be on the teacher who is responsible for making plans with or without help from the school system.

Before you write your long-range plan, you should not only review the materials that the school system provides, but you should also become familiar with the music textbooks that will be available to you and your students. Some publishers designate a minimum music program. A symbol is used to indicate which songs, listening selections, and activities must be covered if students are to progress. It is conceivable that this minimum program could become your long-range plan. However, experienced teachers usually prefer to write their own long-range plans, using curriculum guides, courses of study, and textbooks as resource materials.

The following is a sample long-range plan outlining work for one semester. It is intended for eight- and nine-year-olds who have music classes for thirty minutes twice a week.

SEPTEMBER

Singing Improve posture to promote good tone quality.
Improve diction.

Playing Play quarter and eighth notes from notation. Select rhythm instruments of appropriate tone colors to accompany songs.
Play stepwise melodic fragments on resonator bells to accompany songs.

Listening Recognize the sound of the clarinet.
Recognize changes in tempo.
Recognize ABA form.

Moving Interpret duration of quarter and eighth notes.
Interpret changes in tempo.
Interpret ABA form.

Creating Use rhythm instruments of different tone colors to improvise in ABA form.

OCTOBER

Singing Improve tone quality, continuing to work on good posture and legato singing.
Continue to work toward good diction.
Improve the ability to sing with dynamic control.

Playing Continue playing quarter and eighth notes from notation, adding new combinations and eighth and quarter rests.
Improve the ability to use dynamic controls in playing melody and rhythm instruments.
Play stepwise melodic fragments on bells.

Listening Recognize meter in 2 and 3.
Recognize the sound of the trumpet.

Moving Interpret meter in 2 and 3.
Interpret duration of quarter and eighth notes.

Creating Improvise pieces in 2 and 3 meter.
Improvise in ABA form.

NOVEMBER

Singing Practice songs for a Thanksgiving program.
Become aware of ABA form, repeated patterns, and the need for changes in dynamics.

Playing Practice percussion and bell accompaniments for the Thanksgiving program.
Become aware of major and minor modes, upward and downward direction, and harmonic changes.

Listening Recognize the sound of the flute.

Moving Practice dances for the Thanksgiving program.

Creating Create dances and rhythm instrument accompaniments for the Thanksgiving program.

DECEMBER

Singing Practice songs for a holiday program.
Become familiar with polyphony and with call and response.

Playing Practice accompaniments for the holiday program.
Become familiar with melodic intervals and with harmonic progressions.

Listening Review the sounds of the clarinet, flute, and trumpet.

Moving Practice dances for the holiday program.

Creating Create dances and accompaniments for the holiday program.

JANUARY

Singing Emphasize musical phrasing.
Begin two-part singing.
Continue working toward better control of dynamics.

Playing Begin recorder playing.
Play resonator bells to accompany singing.
Continue to play quarter and eighth notes from notation in a variety of combinations.
Play half notes from notation.
Work on dynamic control when playing melody and rhythm instruments.

Listening Recognize the sound of the trombone.
Recognize meter in 2 and 3.
Recognize ABA form in more complex music.

Moving Interpret meter in 2 and 3.
Interpret duration of quarter, eighth, and half notes.

Creating Compose a piece for recorder using G, A, B, C, and D in quarter and eighth note durations. Use either 2 or 3 meter.

A long-range plan is an overview of what you expect your students to accomplish in a year or in a semester. You are not yet ready to walk into the classroom and teach, however, for you have not planned specifically how much time you will devote to each learning and activity, nor have you selected the materials you will use. You will begin to do this in your short-range plan, which will include both short-range goals and instructional objectives. The long-range and short-range plans can be used as guideposts along the way, since unexpected circumstances may require changes, perhaps like those described earlier in this chapter in regard to modifying lesson plans. Even though plans will often need to be adapted, it has been proven over and over that writing out your goals and objectives greatly improves your chances of success. Written goals and objectives also help to insure a balanced program, avoiding the pitfall of spending too much time on one type of music, or one type of activity, or one element of music, so that your students are given only a limited approach to music.

SHORT-RANGE PLANS

When you write a short-range plan, you take one block of time from the long-range plan and indicate in greater detail what will be taught in each class period within that block of time. Some teachers organize their short-range plans into units to be taught. The teacher who devised the sample long-range plan on pages 68–69 chose to organize the plan by the month. This is what the short-range plan for the month of January looks like:

JANUARY 4 *REVIEW:*

Sing "Oh, Won't You Sit Down?" (page 75).
Sing "Ging Gong Gooli" (page 22).

NEW:

Introduction to recorder.
Rules for handling the recorder.
Playing B, A, and G.
Recorder part for "Ging Gong Gooli" (page 75).

JANUARY 8 *REVIEW:*

Sing "Ging Gong Gooli" (page 22).
Review recorder part (page 75).
Sing "Oh, Won't You Sit Down?" (page 75).

NEW:

Recorder part for "Oh, Won't You Sit Down?" (page 76).
Hand jive for 2 and 3 meter.
Play echo games in 2 and 3 meter using B, A, and G.

JANUARY 11 *REVIEW:*

Sing "Ging Gong Gooli" (page 22).
Review recorder part (page 75).
Sing "Oh, Won't You Sit Down?" (page 75).
Review recorder part (page 76).
Sing "When the Saints Go Marching In " (page 72).

NEW:

Recorder part for "When the Saints Go Marching In" (page 72).

JANUARY 15 *REVIEW:*

Sing "Ging Gong Gooli" (page 22).
Review recorder part (page 75).
Sing "Oh, Won't You Sit Down?" (page 75).
Review recorder part (page 76).
Sing "When the Saints Go Marching In" (page 72).
Review recorder part (page 72).

NEW:

Recorder: C and D.
Play echo games using G, A, B, C, D.

JANUARY 18 *REVIEW:*

Sing "When the Saints Go Marching In" (page 72).
Listen to the recorder part (page 72).
Sing "Little David, Play on Your Harp" (page 73).

NEW:

Have Mr. Downs demonstrate the trombone. (Tape record
   the demonstration.)

JANUARY 22 *REVIEW:*

Sing "Oh, Won't You Sit Down?" (page 75).
Play recorder part (page 76).
Sing "Brother Noah" (page 17).
Sing "Little David, Play on Your Harp" (page 73).

NEW:

Recorder parts for "Little David, Play on Your Harp" (page 73).
Play echo game in 2 and 3 meter using G, A, B, C, D in quarter,
   eighth, and half note durations

JANUARY 25 *REVIEW:*

Sing "Little David, Play on Your Harp" (page 73).
Review recorder parts (page 73).

NEW:

Recorder part for "Brother Noah" (page 73).
Assign students to small groups to write a piece in 2 or 3 meter.
   Use quarter and eighth notes. Use either rhythm instruments
   or any or all of these five tones for recorder: G, A, B, C, D.

Continue to work in groups if necessary.
Hear group reports.
Play tape of trumpet and trombone demonstration. Have students listen
to tape and identify instruments by sound.

WHEN THE SAINTS GO MARCHING IN BLACK SPIRITUAL

2. Oh, when the stars refuse to shine, . . .

3. Oh, when I hear that trumpet sound, . . .

Recorder or Bells

LITTLE DAVID, PLAY ON YOUR HARP

BLACK SPIRITUAL

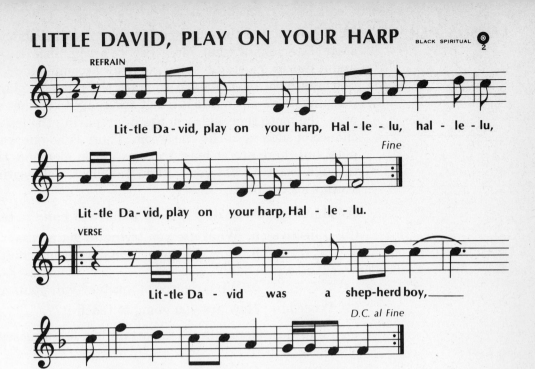

Lit-tle Da-vid, play on your harp, Hal-le-lu, hal-le-lu,

Lit-tle Da-vid, play on your harp, Hal-le-lu.

Lit-tle Da-vid was a shep-herd boy,____

He killed Go-li-ath and shout-ed for joy.

Recorder Parts for "Little David, Play on Your Harp" (Refrain)

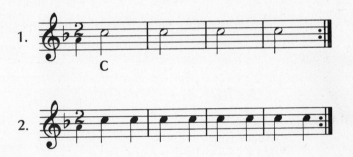

Recorder Part for "Brother Noah"

REFRAIN

LESSON PLANS

The lesson plan is the most specific, most detailed plan you can write. It is a clear statement of what you expect to accomplish in a single class period, and it provides a step-by-step guide for accomplishing it. Some beginning teachers have been known to start their lesson plans with "Say 'good morning' to class." While it is not necessary to be that detailed in a lesson plan, the more thorough you are in preparing the lesson, the better your chance of success in the classroom. There is no one way to write a lesson plan, but there are at least three essential elements that help you think through exactly what you will do in a class, and writing them down will serve as a reminder.

(1) **Materials:** What do you need to have at hand to teach this lesson?

(2) **Objectives: a.** What are you trying to get across?
   b. How will your students let you know they have mastered it?
   c. What degree of mastery will you accept?

(3) **Procedure:** How are you going to teach it?

Two more elements are important in a learning segment (one or more lessons).

(4) **Summary:** Have the students mastered the main points of the learning experience?

(5) **Lead-on:** Are students motivated to move on to next steps? What will you teach next?

Returning to the teacher who prepared the sample long- and short-range plans, this is what the plan for January 8 finally looks like:

JANUARY 8

Materials Music books
Recording
Recorder
Large recorder fingering chart

Concepts *Melody* Tones can move by steps or by leaps. A melody can have repeated tones.
Rhythm Some music has meter in 2. Some music has meter in 3. Some sounds last for one beat. Sometimes there are two sounds for one beat.
Form In ABA form, the first and third sections are alike. The second section is different.

Objectives 1. Play B, A, and G on the recorder, both in isolation and as an accompaniment to songs, accurately and in tempo.
2. Create hand jives in 2 and 3 meter.

Entry Behavior This class has had one lesson on recorder. They have successfully played bells in stepwise passages and can read quarter and eighth notes. Academically the students are at and above grade level.

Procedure Have the class sing "Ging Gong Gooli" (page 22).
Teach motions to give students a feeling for steady beat and meter. (See Chapter 2, page 22.)
Have the class study the recorder part for "Ging Gong Gooli."

Recorder Part for "Ging Gong Gooli"

Ask the class to show the quarter- and eighth-note rhythms of the recorder part by saying "ta ta, ti ti ti ti," or "one two, one and two and." Have them say the letter names of the notes.

Have the class finger the part as they "say" the rhythm.

Have the class finger the part as they sing it (sing letter names and say "rest" where appropriate). Observe repeats.

Have the class play the part.

Have the class play the part with the recording or piano or voice.

Have the class sing "Oh, Won't You Sit Down?"

OH, WON'T YOU SIT DOWN? BLACK SPIRITUAL

B VERSE

SOLO

1. Who's that yon - der dressed in red? __

CHORUS

Must be the chil - dren that __ Mo - ses led. __

SOLO

Who's that yon - der dressed in white? __

CHORUS

Must be the chil - dren of the Is - rael - ite. __

2. Who's that yonder dressed in blue?

Must be the children that are comin' through.

Who's that yonder dressed in black?

Must be the hypocrites a-turnin' back. *Refrain*

Have the class study the recorder part, identifying steps and leaps. The recorder part begins on the word *sit*.

Recorder Part for "Oh, Won't You Sit Down?"

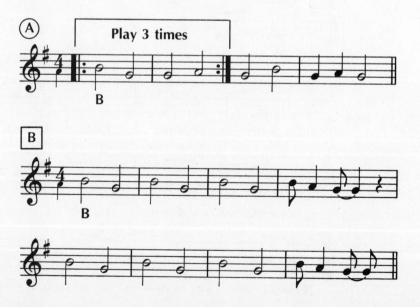

Follow the same procedure as for "Ging Gong Gooli."

Have the class identify words of the song that correspond with the following pattern in section B — "Moses Led" and "Israelite."

Have students clap that rhythm and sing the letter names of the tones in the pattern.

Have students play the recorder parts for sections A and B.

Review the meaning of *D.C. al Fine*.

Have students recall other songs using *D.C. al Fine* and ABA form.

Have the class play the recorder part with the recording or piano.

Review B, A, and G by playing an echo game in 2 or 3 meter:

Have students take turns as leader in the echo game.

Ask students how the echo game could be played to make an ABA form.

Tell students that in the next lesson they will learn to play a recorder part for one of their favorite songs.

Perhaps there should be a word of caution before leaving the subject of lesson plans. If you are honest with yourself and fair to your students, you must have a lesson plan when you go into the classroom. However, once inside the classroom you cannot let the lesson plan be more important than the needs of your students. There will be times when you need to modify your plan. There will be times when students ask important questions that, although they are not in the plan, are relevant to what is being studied. You should never dismiss an important question or cut off a relevant discussion because it is not provided for in the plan. Such questions and discussions are important because they help you learn more about your students' concerns and interests, and they encourage the participation of students who have something meaningful to say. By all means, you should not let the class wander off on irrelevant discussions, but when the students have something pertinent to contribute, you should give them the opportunity to do so. The plan will still be there for the next class session, but a student whose desire to contribute something worthwhile is ignored may never volunteer again.

GENERALIZATIONS

The following generalizations may be drawn from the discussion of planning.

Students Teachers must know as much as possible about their students so that they can plan lessons that will interest and challenge each of them.

Materials Teachers must be familiar with a variety of materials, or know where to find them. The more materials teachers have at hand, the better they will be able to plan lessons that will meet the needs and interests of each child in their classes.

Activities Teachers must learn to guide as many different kinds of activities as possible, so that they can change activities as frequently as necessary to keep the lesson moving at an interesting pace.

Music Teachers must know their subject. They must know as much as possible about the inner workings of music so that they can plan valid musical experiences for their students.

Plans 1. Teachers must have a general overview of what they intend to accomplish during the year (long-range plan, or program objectives).
2. Teachers must know exactly what they intend to teach in a month or six weeks (short-range plans, or instructional objectives).
3. Teachers must know how they will present material in each class session (lesson plans with behavioral and instructional objectives).

Objectives Teachers must remember to state the specific objectives of each lesson in terms that will make it possible to measure or observe mastery on the part of each student.

Attitude Teachers must use common sense. They must remember that everything that occurs within a class period cannot be predetermined in a lesson plan. Teachers must not hesitate to "forget" the plan when circumstances require it.

ASSESSMENT 1 Study each of the following plans. Decide whether the plan
a. is an example of a long-range plan, a short-range plan, or a lesson plan;
b. states objectives in behavioral terms;
c. provides for a variety of activities;
d. provides for a balance between knowledge and skill development; and
e. provides for valid musical experiences.

PLAN ONE

Materials Textbook
Record player
Record
Rhythm instruments

Objective Understand rondo form.

Procedure   Have students sing "Mama Don't 'Low" (page 42). Have half the class clap the steady beat as others clap the rhythm of the words.

Have students sing the refrain of "Wade in the Water" (page 39).

Select one or two students to play the rhythm of the words on tambourines as others slap their thighs on the steady beat.

Have the class sing one verse and refrain of "The Drunken Sailor" (page 29).

Select a few students to play the rhythm of the words on triangles as others snap their fingers to the steady beat.

Explain that composers sometimes take three ideas (usually tunes) and put them together to create a composition in rondo form. Then have students create a composition in rondo form by putting together a rhythm accompaniment for the three songs they have just sung. No one will sing aloud. Only instruments and clapping will be heard in this "Rondo for Percussion and Clapping."

Section A: "Mama Don't 'Low" — half the class clapping the steady beat, the other half clapping the rhythm of the words

Section B: "Wade in the Water" — tambourines playing the rhythm of the words, others slapping thighs on the steady beat

Section A: Same as before

Section C: "The Drunken Sailor" — triangles playing the rhythm of the words, others snapping fingers on the steady beat

Section A: Same as before

Ask for four volunteers to create movement for section A, using only jerky movements like a robot or a machine. Suggest that they move only their heads, for example, or only their arms, legs, or shoulders.

Ask for four more volunteers to create movement for section B. Suggest that they stay in one place, bending and stretching in different ways, such as backward, forward, up, down, low, high.

Ask for four other volunteers to act out section C. Suggest that they walk in different ways, such as forward, backward, or sideways; with heavy steps or light steps.

Perform the "dance" in rondo form accompanied by the "Rondo for Percussion and Clapping" described above.

Write directions on the chalkboard as follows:

Section A: "Mama Don't 'Low" — clapping, jerky motions

Section B: "Wade in the Water" — slapping and tambourines, bending and stretching

Section A: Same as before

Section C: "The Drunken Sailor" — snapping and triangles, walking

Section A: Same as before

Put the information in *Call Chart: Rondo* on the chalkboard. (See page 81.)

CALL CHART: Rondo

CALL CHART: Rondo ⊚₂

1. SECTION A	TRUMPET SOLO; FOUR PHRASES — PHRASES 1 AND 3 ARE EXACTLY ALIKE, PHRASES 2 AND 4 ARE NEARLY ALIKE.	
2. SECTION B	NO TRUMPET; TWO PHRASES, ALIKE IN RHYTHM AND MELODY	
3. SECTION A	PHRASES 3 AND 4 ONLY	
4. SECTION C	NO TRUMPET; LONG AND SHORT PHRASES	
5. SECTION A	SAME AS NUMBER 1	

Ask students to observe the order of the sections as listed on the page. Is there anything familiar about the order? (Yes, it is the same as the rhythm rondo.)

Ask students to listen to section A as they follow the music. Ask which instruments they can recognize. Ask how many phrases there are in section A. This should take about three or four listenings.

Have students follow *Call Chart: Rondo* as they listen to the entire rondo.

Review the meaning of the term *rondo*. Add it to the music vocabulary list.

PLAN TWO

By the end of _____ most children in this class will be able to
1. demonstrate by some form of movement that they can identify changes of tempo in the music they hear and sing;
2. use the text or melody of a song to determine what dynamics should be used in its performance;
3. identify theme and variations form in recorded music;
4. read, perform, and identify (by their sound) two rhythm patterns both in isolation and in songs.

PLAN THREE

Materials   Record player
Recording
Resonator bells

Objective   (First-grade class)
Demonstrate ability to hear downward direction in melodies by moving bodies in a downward direction and by playing step bells appropriately.

Procedure   Review "Little Bird, Go Through My Window" (page 82).

LITTLE BIRD, GO THROUGH MY WINDOW

FOLK SONG
FROM SOUTH CAROLINA

TRANSCRIBED AND ADAPTED FROM THE LIBRARY OF CONGRESS FIELD RECORDING AFS 1303

Lively

1. Lit-tle bird, lit-tle bird, Go through my win-dow. Lit-tle bird, lit-tle bird,
2. Blue - bird, blue - bird, Blue - bird, blue - bird,

Go through my win-dow. Lit-tle bird, lit-tle bird, Go through my win-dow an'
Blue - bird, blue - bird,

buy mo-las-ses can-dy. Go through my win-dow, my sug-ar lump, Go

through my win-dow, my sug-ar lump, An' buy mo-las-ses can-dy.

Play a game. Form a large circle, holding hands. Hold hands high to make "windows." Choose one or two children to be "little birds." As the song is sung, the little birds go in and out the windows. On "buy molasses candy," children crouch down with hands still joined so that the little birds cannot go through the windows.

Have children go to their places and sing the song. Ask them to clap during the downward passage so you may be sure they have identified it.

Make your own "step bells." Use resonator bells D, E, F#, G, and A. Arrange books, blocks of wood, or other readily available materials to show relative highness and lowness. Put D on the lowest step, E on the next highest (to the right of D), and so on. Show children how to play the descending pattern on "buy molasses candy" at the end of the song (A, G, F#, E, D).

Have children play the part as it occurs in the song.

Have children sing "I'm Gonna Sing" (page 9).

Place resonator bells on the "steps" in this order, left to right: G, A, B, C.

Identify the downward passage at the end of the song.

Have children play the descending melody of "And obey the spirit of the Lord" on the bells.

Chorus Rehearsal

MARCH 1

Review: "Waters Ripple and Flow"

WATERS RIPPLE AND FLOW   FOLK SONG FROM CZECHOSLOVAKIA   ENGLISH WORDS BY MARGARET FISHBACK

Call attention to recurring rhythm patterns.

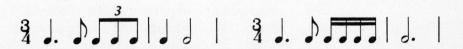

Call attention to the change of key.
Work on phrasing.
Work on legato singing.

New: "Bidin' My Time"
Call attention to syncopation.
Note ABA form with coda.
Note dynamic markings.
"Green, Green"
Work on part-singing (refrain only).
Call attention to the dotted rhythm.

MARCH 8

Review: "Bidin' My Time"
Work on the vowel *i* in the words *bidin'* and *time*.
"Waters Ripple and Flow"
Work on phrasing.

New: "Dona Nobis Pacem"
Call attention to large skips in the melody; prepare for them by practicing exercises that incorporate large skips.
Practice only in unison.

MARCH 15

Review: "Green, Green"
Work on part-singing.
"Bidin' My Time"
Work on soft but vibrant singing.
"Waters Ripple and Flow"
Work on good attacks and releases.
"Dona Nobis Pacem"
Continue to work on singing in unison.

New: "Dona Nobis Pacem"
Have students create a dance.

MARCH 27

Review: "Bidin' My Time"
Work on section B only.
"Waters Ripple and Flow"
Work on dynamics.
"Dona Nobis Pacem"
More support on high tones.

New: "Green, Green"
Introduce the verse.
Work on attention to conductor.

ASSESSMENT 2 Write a lesson plan for a class that meets for thirty minutes twice a week. Include the following information:
a. age level of the students;
b. background or experiences the students would need to be successful (part of the long-range and short-range plans); and
c. how this lesson relates to the long-range and short-range plans.

ASSESSMENT 3 The following plans[2] are for Grades 1, 3, and 5 having music once a week. Explain how these plans show

a. that music concepts are being developed;

b. a continuous growth in ability to conceptualize;

c. growth in musical skills.

GRADE 1

Week I "All Around the Kitchen"
Feeling the steady beat
Patting lap, playing rhythm sticks and drum

Week II "Skip to My Lou"
Steady beat — fast and slow
Playing tambourine

Week III "This Old Man"
Melodic direction — upward, downward

Week IV "Barnacle Bill" and "Bye'm Bye"
Meter: beats that move in sets of 3
High-to-low leap in "Bye'm Bye"

Week V "Michael, Row the Boat Ashore"
Form — call and response
Phrases

Week VI "The Wind Blew East"
Music that has beat or no beat
Contrast in music — find what is different
Repetition (sameness)

Weeks VII and VIII "I'm Gonna Sing" and "Raise a Ruckus"
Style — Black spiritual; lullaby
Dynamics — loud and soft

GRADE 3

Week 1 "Brother Noah"
Melodic direction
Upward, downward, scalewise

Week II "Old Joe Clark"
Form — sections of a song: AB
Melody — the tune
Accompaniment — tone color
Style — country-western

Week III "Mama Paquita"
Melodic direction
Style — folk song

Week IV "Ain't Gonna Rain"
Tone color — bass fiddle
Style — country-western
Meter in 2 (duple)

---

[2]Courtesy of Marian Bruscusco, Music Teacher, Baltimore City Public Schools.

Week V "Find the Ring"
        Meter in 3 (triple)

Week VI "The Ghost of John"
        Dynamics — loud (*forte*), soft (*piano*); gradually getting softer, gradually
           getting louder
        Tone color — electronic synthesizer

Week VII "Che Che Koolay"
        Form — call and response

Week VIII "Bella Bimba"
        Register — high and low

GRADE 5

Week 1 (REVIEW)
"Mama Don't 'Low"
        Tempo — fast or slow, movement
        Meter — duple or triple
        Style — rock, folk, gospel, chorale, dance, pop, spiritual, country, hymn

Week II "I'm Gonna Walk"
        Staccato — short detached sounds
"Old Texas"
        Legato — long, connected sounds
        Coda — an added ending to a song
        Ostinato — a pattern repeated throughout a song
        Rests and notes — quarter, whole, half, eighth
        Fermata — a "hold"

Week III "Emma"
        Style — rock, spiritual, calypso
        Outstanding characteristic of calypso music — syncopation
        Repetition — melody pattern or rhythm pattern that is repeated
        Contrast — melody or rhythm patterns that are different from previous
           patterns
        Texture — thick or thin

Week IV "Mineira de Minas"
        Style — Spanish folk song
        Form — the shape of the song by sections, A and B
        Change of meter — section A triple, section B duple

Week V "Sunny Lane"
        Form — ABAB
        Style — contemporary popular
        D.C. al Fine — go back to the beginning and sing to the *Fine*
        First ending, second ending
        Tone color — the instruments that suggest a particular idea (in this case,
           "rain" — electric bass)

ASSESSMENT 4 What are the strengths and weaknesses of the following form used in writing lesson plans?[3]

```
LESSON PLAN                          Date of Lesson_____
                                     School_____
MUSIC                                No. of Pupils_____
                                     Grade_____


OBJECTIVES: LONG RANGE _____
_____
_____
_____


OBJECTIVES: SHORT RANGE _____
_____
_____
_____


PROCEDURES _____
_____
_____
_____
_____
_____
_____
_____


MATERIALS_____
_____
_____
_____


EVALUATION_____
_____
_____
_____
_____
_____
_____
_____
_____
_____
_____
_____
```

[3]Courtesy of Robert Fleecs, Music Teacher, Baltimore City Public Schools.

5

Using Deductive and Inductive Approaches

CHAPTER OBJECTIVE   *Describe the inductive and deductive approaches to teaching. Give an example of each.*

Most children bring to school a natural enthusiasm for music, an eagerness to sing and to play instruments. However, children's natural enthusiasm is one thing; keeping it alive and growing is quite another. This can pose some serious problems for the teacher. To increase children's interest in music, deepen their understanding of it, and help them develop maximum musical sensitivity, it is imperative that the teacher know *how* to teach music most effectively.

Basically, there are two approaches to teaching, the deductive (explaining) and the inductive (questioning). Both approaches are valid, and successful teachers usually draw on both. Even so, the deductive approach has generally been overworked, despite the teachers' complaint that "students never seem to remember what has just been explained to them."

THE INDUCTIVE APPROACH

The inductive approach moves through a series of experiences from the specific to the general. A teacher using the inductive approach asks questions designed to lead students to determine for themselves the concept or generalization being taught. For example, if the inductive approach is used to teach a lesson about the grouping of steady beats, the teacher asks the children to tap the steady beat as they sing "Ging Gong Gooli" (page 22). If children have difficulty, the teacher might ask, "Can you walk to the beat of this music?" And then, "Can you move the beat from your feet to your hands and tap it?" The teacher then selects a child to lead the class in tapping the steady beat as they sing "Ging Gong Gooli," perhaps offering a rhythm instrument to play.

When the children have succeeded in tapping the steady beat, the teacher might say, "Let's change tapping to clapping and keep time to 'Ging Gong Gooli' again, but this time, can you keep time without clapping every single beat?" As the students clap, the teacher looks for a child who is clapping only on the strong (stressed) beats — the first beat of each measure — and asks that child to lead the class in this new way of keeping time to the music.

Now that they are able to discern the steady beat and the strong beats in "Ging Gong Gooli," the children are ready to complete the final step necessary to identify the concept — putting the two activities together. The teacher divides the class in half, instructing one half to tap the steady beat of "Ging Gong Gooli" while the other half claps only the strong beats. Appointing a leader for each half of the class, the teacher gives each leader a different kind of percussion instrument to play — for example, sticks to lead the tapping of the steady beat and a drum to lead the clapping of the strong beats — so that the students can clearly distinguish the sound of the strong beat from the sound of the steady beat. After the class has had some success with this activity, the teacher asks questions, such as "If you say 'One' every time the drum sounds, how will you count to this music?" Or "Who will go to the chalkboard and draw a tall (vertical) mark for each drum sound and a short mark for each sound the sticks make between the drum sounds? Is there a pattern in the drawing? Are there sets of two or sets of three?" After the children have come to realize that the beats in "Ging Gong Gooli" and some other songs they know are grouped in sets of two, the teacher continues in the same way to lead the children to realize that beats can also be grouped in sets of three.

As the teacher you should remember three things when using the inductive approach. First, you must be very careful to keep the class on the right track. For example, in the sample teaching procedure the teacher asks if there is a pattern in the drawing of the tall and short marks on the chalkboard. If a child should answer that there is no pattern because some of the marks are crooked, the teacher must reject that answer. The teacher cannot let anything divert the children from seeing the pattern of tall and short marks that represents beats grouped in sets of two.

Second, you should remember that young children will need many, many experiences with a musical concept, or generalization, before they have the background to compare, contrast, categorize, and conceptualize. (See "Theories of Child Growth and Development," page 195.)

Third, while the main feature of the inductive approach is that it places responsibility on the students to arrive logically at the desired conclusion, you must not feel that you cannot help students if they are having difficulty. If students do not have sufficient background to follow your line of questioning, you must slip into the role of "teller" to ensure that the students understand the lesson you are teaching.

Here is another example of the inductive approach:

Concept Some melodies outline chords.

Objectives 1. Identify chords outlined in a melody.
2. Improvise a melody based on the C, F, and G chords.

Procedure • As John strums the C chord on the Autoharp, hum any pitch that you hear.
• Keep humming your pitch, and change as John strums a different chord.

Select three capable students. Give each a resonator bell that plays one tone of the C chord (C, E, G). As the class hums with the Autoharp, have the bells played individually and in succession. Encourage the bell players to change the order, use repeated tones, and so on. Follow the same procedure with the

F chord (F, A, C) and the G chord (G, B, D). Encourage bell players to experiment with different ordering, using different rhythm patterns and other variations.

ANOTHER DAY
- Do you remember that in the last lesson most of you had a chance to play resonator bells with the Autoharp chords? You played them differently than we had played them before. In what way did we play them differently? (One at a time, not as chords)
- Today others will have a chance to play bells, but I am going to give you a special rhythm pattern to play. Here it is.

Put the following rhythm pattern on the chalkboard and have students clap it.

- Will three students in the first row come and get the bells for the C chord?

Assign bells to form the C, F, and G chords. Have bell players stand in a line in this order: C, E, G,   F, A, C,   G, B, D.

- Michael, will you play the Autoharp chords in this order: C chord, F chord, G chord? Class, will you hum along with Michael? Keep repeating those chords. Class, be sure to listen to the Autoharp and always match one of the tones you hear.

Some children may have difficulty with this, but the activity will focus attention on the chord tones. Be sure that the Autoharp chords are louder than the humming.

- That was good. This time the bells will play along with you. Each group will play their chord from the low pitch to the high pitch. The C-chord group will play their pattern once, then the F-chord group, and so forth. They will play one pitch at a time and use the rhythm pattern we just clapped. They will play each pattern once and then we will move on to the next pattern. Everyone else, find your tone and hum with the Autoharp.

Write the directions on a chart or the chalkboard. The melody should sound like the beginning of "Matilda."

MATILDA   FOLK SONG FROM JAMAICA

1. Five thou-sand dol-lars, friend, I lost. The wo-man e-ven take me cart and horse._ Ma-til-da, she take me mon-ey and run Ven-e-zue-la. _____

2. My money was to buy me house and land,
   The woman she got a serious plan.
   Matilda, she take me money and run Venezuela.
   Refrain

3. Now the money was safe in me bed,
   Stuck in the pillow beneath me head,
   But Matilda, she find me money and run Venezuela.
   Refrain

4. Never will I love again,
   All me money gone in vain
   'Cause Matilda, she take me money and run Venezuela.
   Refrain

Give several students an opportunity to play the resonator bells. Repetition will help the children remember the tune.

In using the inductive approach, here are samples of the kinds of questions you will ask your students.

1. *Questions that require recall*
- You did that very well. Listen to this song. I believe you will find that you already know some of it. Which parts have you heard before?

Play the recording of "Matilda" (page 90, record 2).

2. *Questions that require comparison*
- Did you remember any part of the song? (Yes)
- Which part? (The four "Matildas")
- How did you happen to know that part? (We played it on bells.)
- What tones did you use? (Tones in the C, F, and G chords)
- Have you ever used those tones before? (Yes, as chordal accompaniments to songs)

3. *Questions that require contrasting*
- How were those tones used differently in the song we just played? (As part of the melody)

4. *Questions that require categorizing*

- Let's see if you can find other songs that have patterns of chord tones as part of the melody. You remember "Sambalele." Clap the rhythm of the first phrase. What chord tones did we use to play the first part of the first phrase? (F, A, C)
- Play the chord tones using the rhythm that we clapped. Can you make the tones sound like the melody in the first part of the phrase? (Yes)
- Turn to "Sambalele" in your book. Check the first part of the phrase. Does the melody use the tones of the F chord? (Yes)
- Do you find it in another place in the song? (Yes, at the beginning of the third phrase)

In subsequent lessons have students check other songs, such as "Ging Gong Gooli" (page 22), "The Drunken Sailor" (page 29), and "Sasa Akroma" (page 31). It will be useful to have a chord chart, such as the one on page 194, posted so that students can readily check the tones of each chord.

5. *Questions that require conceptualizing or generalizing*

- After studying all these songs and studying the chord chart, what have you learned about melodies? (Melodies sometimes outline chords.)

If you decided to pursue this concept beyond the point where students are able to make the generalization, you could then continue with the following three steps.

6. *Questions that help analyze*

- Are any melodies made up entirely of chord tones?
- Do any of these songs rely on only two tones of the chord?
- What are they?

7. *Questions that help synthesize*

- If you were going to create a melody using chord tones, how much of your melody would be made up of chord tones?
- Would you have any places in the melody that only hint at chords?
- Would you use repeated rhythm patterns?
- Would you choose a poem and fit your melody to it?

8. *Questions that help evaluate*

- Think of a particular musical idea — rhythmic, melodic, or harmonic — that you would use if you were composing a song.

In both examples where the inductive approach is used to teach a musical concept, the concept grows out of experiences that can be (1) remembered, (2) compared, (3) contrasted, (4) categorized, and (5) generalized. In each step the students can refer to experiences they have had, and it is their responsibility to arrive at the generalizations.

THE DEDUCTIVE APPROACH

When a teacher uses the deductive approach to teach a musical concept, the teacher states the concept and explains how it applies to a specific piece of music, then asks the students to do the same thing. For example, if the lesson is about the grouping of steady beats, the teacher tells the class that steady beats are sometimes grouped in sets of two and sometimes in sets of three, and that the top number of the meter signature indicates how the beats are grouped. Then, turning to a specific song — for example, "Ging Gong Gooli" (page 22) — the teacher calls attention to the 2 in the meter signature and asks the children to sing the song and perhaps move to the beat to confirm that the beats are grouped in sets of two. Finally, the teacher asks the students to repeat the concept, along with the information about the top number of the meter signature, and to look in their books for other songs that have beats in sets of two. The teacher follows the same procedure with songs in triple meter.

Here is another sample lesson with the same song and content that was used to illustrate the inductive approach. This plan uses a deductive approach.

Concept Some melodies outline chords.

Objectives 1. Identify chords outlined in a melody.
2. Improvise a melody based on the C, F, and G chords.

Procedure • Some songs we have sung have one interesting thing in common. They use the tones of chords as parts of their melodies. We have played chords on resonator bells and on the Autoharp to accompany our singing, and you have learned what tones make up the C, F, and G chords. Study the chord markings in the song "Matilda." Do you see the C chord marked over the first "Matilda"?
• Look at the notes at the beginning of the melody (C, E, G). They spell out the C chord. Now look at the second "Matilda,". . .

Pinpoint each place where a chord outlines the melody.

• We are going to test the idea that some melodies outline chords by playing the beginning of the song. Play C, then E, then G.
• Now play C, E, and G together.
• Are the chord tones the same as the melody? (Yes)
• Let's look at another song in our book to see whether the melody outlines chords. Turn to "The Drunken Sailor."
• Do you find chords outlined in the melody of this song? (Yes)
• John, will you play the chords for "The Drunken Sailor" on the Autoharp?

D min.	D min.	D min.	D min.
C	C	C	C
D min.	D min.	D min.	D min.
D min.	A min.	D min.	D min.
			(repeat)

Have students improvise melodies that outline chords. (Use the procedure in which the same concept was taught with the inductive approach, page 89.) Have students point out places where the melody outlines a chord.

• What do some of the melodies you studied have in common? (Some melodies outline chords.)

In the deductive approach, it is the responsibility of the teacher to state the concept, illustrate it by using a specific example, have students give other examples, and have students restate the concept.

Most successful teachers use a combination of deductive (telling) and inductive (asking) approaches in nearly every lesson. Here is an example of a combination of the two approaches.

Concept A melody can be made of repeated phrases and contrasting phrases.

Objective Create a piece that has repeating and contrasting phrases.

Procedure Teach the following song by rote.[1]

DEEP BLUE SEA AMERICAN FOLK SONG

phrase 1
1. Deep blue sea, ba - by, deep blue sea,

phrase 2
Deep blue sea, ba - by, deep blue sea,

phrase 3
Deep blue sea, ba - by, deep blue sea,

phrase 4
It was Wil - lie_____ what got drown - ded

In the deep blue sea.

2. Low'r him down with a golden chain, *(3 times)*
   It was Willie . . .

3. Dig his grave with a silver spade, *(3 times)*

4. Wrap him up in a silken shroud, *(3 times)*

5. Golden sun bring him back to me, *(3 times)*

- There are several ways phrases may be alike or different. Let's make a list of them. One way is to have the same or a different melody. Listen to one phrase of "Deep Blue Sea" as I hum it. Which phrase did I hum? (Phrase 1)
- Is the same tune used again in another phrase? (Yes, in phrase 3)
- Here is phrase 2. Is there another phrase like it? (No)
- We are going to discover other ways in which phrases are alike and different, and list them on the chalkboard. What shall we say about the melody? (Some phrases are repeated, and some are contrasting.)

[1]See Hints for Teaching Rote Songs, p. 186.

- Listen again to the recording of the song. This time, notice places where the singers pause. Raise your hand each time you hear a silence in the voices. The silences come at the ends of phrases.
- Everyone stand and walk toward the front of the room. Freeze each time you hear a silence at the end of a phrase. Start to walk again at the beginning of the next phrase.
- Did you walk the same distance for each phrase? (No)
- Which phrases were alike in length? (Phrases 1, 2, and 3)
- Which phrase was different? (4) How was it different? (It was longer.)
- What shall we write on our list about the lengths of phrases? (The phrases in this song are of the same and different lengths.)
- John, will you play the Autoharp chords? Don't forget the rests at the ends of phrases.
- What did you notice about the harmony? Do some phrases have the same harmony? (Phrases 1 and 3 are alike. Phrases 2 and 4 are different.)

This may require more than one hearing. If students have trouble recognizing chord progressions and harmony, help them by making a visual aid, such as the following.

G	C	G	G	C	C	G
G	C	G	G	A min.	G	D$_7$
G	C	G	G	C	C	G
G	G	G	G	C	G	D$_7$	G

- What can you say about the order of chords in each phrase? Is the order the same or different? (In some it is the same, and in some it is different.) What shall we list? (In this song some phrases have the same order of chords, and some have a different order of chords.)
- As you sing the song to yourself, clap the rhythm of the words.
- What do you notice about the rhythm of the words of phrases 1, 2, and 3? (The rhythm of the words is the same in all three phrases.)
- What do you notice about the rhythm of the words of phrase 4? (It is different.)
- What can we add to the list we have made on the chalkboard about phrases? (Phrases can have repeated rhythm patterns or different rhythm patterns.)

Summarize the list on the chalkboard with a statement such as this:
> The phrases in a song can have repetition and contrast in melody, length, harmony, and rhythm.

- Here is a phrase that we will use in our next class. Using the ideas listed on the chart, we will combine phrases to form a piece.

In the lesson above, you can find instances where the deductive approach is used. The teacher explains that the melodies of phrases can be the same or different and then demonstrates with examples. The next three activities are approached inductively in that the students' attention is focused on the phrases' length, harmonic structure, and rhythm pattern. The teacher asks students to remember what they have done, to compare and contrast the phrases, and to name the ways in which the phrases are different. Finally, the teacher asks them to generalize about each activity and then formulate a statement about "Deep Blue Sea"; this provides a lead-in for the next class.

GENERALIZATIONS

The following generalizations may be drawn from the discussion of deductive and inductive approaches.

Young Children Young children tend to deal with specific examples. The teacher can help children generalize through comparing, contrasting, and categorizing.

Older Children Older children, when given a generalized statement, can find or create specific examples to prove the statement. They are becoming capable of synthesizing, analyzing, and evaluating.

Approaches Many teaching strategies include both inductive and deductive approaches.

ASSESSMENT 1 Here are outlines of parts of three lesson plans. Study them and decide whether the teacher is using a deductive approach, an inductive approach, or a combination of both.

PLAN ONE

Materials "Row, Row, Row Your Boat"

Objective Identify three different rhythm patterns in a familiar song, and determine that one of the patterns is repeated.

Procedure The teacher states that a song may contain several different rhythm patterns and that some of the patterns may be repeated. The teacher identifies the rhythm patterns in "Row, Row, Row Your Boat."

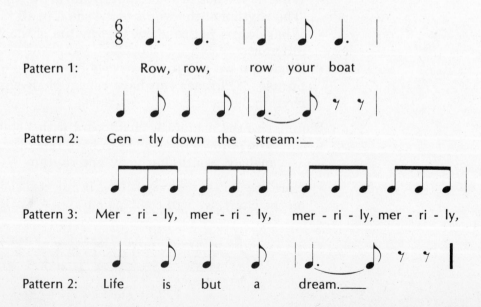

Pattern 1:   Row, row,   row your boat

Pattern 2:   Gen - tly down the   stream:___

Pattern 3:   Mer - ri - ly, mer - ri - ly,   mer - ri - ly, mer - ri - ly,

Pattern 2:   Life   is   but   a   dream.___

The teacher asks half the class to clap only on pattern 1, the other half to clap only on pattern 3, and everyone to clap on pattern 2.

The teacher asks the class what they have learned about rhythm patterns.

PLAN TWO

Materials   "Row, Row, Row Your Boat"

Objective   Identify three different rhythm patterns in a familiar song, and determine that one of the patterns is repeated.

Procedure   The teacher asks three children to clap the rhythm of their names, making certain to call on children whose names have different rhythm patterns.

The teacher writes each child's name and its rhythm pattern on the chalkboard. For example:

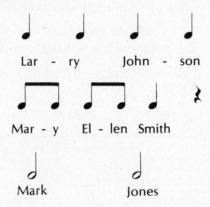

The teacher has the entire class clap the rhythm of the three names.

The teacher asks if there is anyone in the class whose name has the same rhythm as one of those on the board.

The teacher writes the identical patterns next to one another. For example:

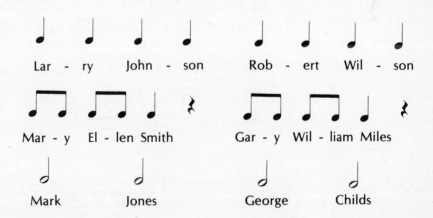

The teacher divides the class into groups of four and instructs them to plan a piece for percussion instruments using the three original patterns plus any one of the identical patterns. The patterns may occur in any order.

The teacher asks each group to perform its piece so that the class can determine which pattern each group has chosen to repeat.

The teacher has the class sing "Row, Row, Row Your Boat," then asks the class how this song is similar to their percussion pieces.

Materials   "Oh, What a Beautiful City" (page 98, record 2)
"Get on Board" (record 1)
"All Night, All Day" (record 1)
Record player
Classroom space for rhythmic activities

Concept   Changing the tempo (rate of speed) of music changes the feeling of the music.

Objectives   1. Sing "Oh, What a Beautiful City" at two different tempos.
2. Recognize the difference in tempo between two unfamiliar songs.
3. Define the word *tempo*.

Procedure   Start the lesson with an activity the class enjoys (for example, echo clapping). Make a game of it by changing from clapping hands to snapping fingers to slapping thighs. Change from fast to slow and from slow to fast.

• That was excellent! We are going to do something different today with a song we know. Lisa, will you read the first sentence on the chart?

Have objectives listed on a chart or the chalkboard. (Omit the word *objectives*.)

• Good, Lisa. You remember that we learned "Oh, What a Beautiful City" in our last lesson. Let's clap the one phrase that we had trouble with. Do you remember which one it was? ("Twelve gates-a to the city")

OH, WHAT A BEAUTIFUL CITY   BLACK SPIRITUAL

Oh,   what   a   beau - ti - ful   cit - y,____

Oh,   what   a   beau - ti - ful   cit - y,____

Oh,   what   a   beau - ti - ful   cit - y,____

Twelve gates - a   to   the cit - y,____   Hal - le - lu - jah!

- ·Good, you corrected the problem. Here is the same song sung in a different way. In what way is it different?

Play version 2 of "Oh, What a Beautiful City," which is sung more slowly.

- Let's sing it more slowly with the record, just as we heard it.
- Good, you can sing this song either fast or slow.
- I am going to play two songs, one right after the other. Keep time to the steady beat. Which one is faster? ("Get on Board" is faster than "All Night, All Day.")
- You are correct! Form a large circle around the outside of the room.
- When you hear my slow drumbeat, walk in time to it. Keep moving in the large circle.
- Good. When I play a fast beat, change the large circle into a large square. Follow each wall and then make a square corner.
- As I play one of the two pieces we just heard, walk to the steady beat. Walk in a square if it is fast, and walk in a circle if it is slow.
- Good. You certainly heard the changes in tempo.

- Let's make a list of what we learned today about fast and slow music. What did we do with "Oh, What a Beautiful City"? (We sang it both fast and slow.)
- Do you think other songs could be sung either fast or slow? (Yes) Then what can we remember about tempo? (Some songs can be sung either fast or slow.)
- Think about the two songs you heard as you walked around the room. How were they different? (One was fast and one was slow.)
- Did the fast one make you feel like moving differently than the slow one? (Yes) Did you move differently? (Yes)
- What could we say about fast and slow music and the way it makes us feel? (Fast music makes us feel different from slow music.)
- Think of a word that tells how fast or how slow we walk, drive a car, or get a job done. (Answers will vary.)
- There is a musical term that tells about fast or slow in music. That word is *tempo*. We will add it to your vocabulary list and in our next class we will write our own definition of the word *tempo*.

ASSESSMENT 2   Describe the differences between the deductive approach and the inductive approach.

ASSESSMENT 3   Write a plan or a portion of a plan that illustrates an inductive approach, a deductive approach, or a combination of the two.

Materials   "Dipidu" (page 100)

Concepts   1. Beats can be organized in sets of two or three.
2. Some pieces use one meter or the other, and some pieces use both.

DIPIDU

FOLK SONG FROM UGANDA   ENGLISH WORDS BY JOAN GILBERT VAN POZNAK

FROM UNICEF BOOK OF CHILDREN'S SONGS. COMPILED AND WITH PHOTOGRAPHS BY WILLIAM I. KAUFMAN. COPYRIGHT 1970 BY WILLIAM I. KAUFMAN. PUBLISHED BY STACKPOLE BOOKS.

Good-day, good-day to you, Good-day, O dip-i-du,

Good-day, good-day to you, Good-day, O dip-i-du.

Dip, dip, dip-i-du, Dip-i-du, O dip-i-du.

Dip, dip, dip dip, dip-i-du, Dip-i-du, O dip-i-du.

6 Teaching Large and Small Groups

CHAPTER OBJECTIVE   *Write a description that contrasts the teacher's role in activities involving large and small groups. Indicate how the teacher*
(a) prepares for the activity,
(b) manages the available time, and
(c) evaluates student achievement.

In this chapter, group activity is defined as any activity that involves several participants. A group activity may involve hundreds of participants, such as a chorus or large audience, or just a few, such as three or four children working out a musical problem together.

LARGE GROUP ACTIVITY

Large group activities in the elementary school include music classes, chorus rehearsals, orchestra rehearsals, assembly sing-alongs, and concerts. In some schools, all these activities are conducted by a music specialist. In others, the music specialist takes care of the chorus and the orchestra and visits the classrooms once or twice a week; the rest of the week, the classroom teacher teaches music. In still other schools, classroom teachers are responsible for the total music program, and if some have had a little extra music training, they may be put in charge of the school chorus. In large group activity the teacher must take charge, leading all activities, making final decisions, and resolving any conflicts that arise. The students are expected to cooperate and to abide by the teacher's decisions.

PURPOSE OF LARGE GROUP ACTIVITY

Large group activity has traditionally been the heart of the school music experience. At its best, the large group music experience — whether in a chorus, an orchestra, a band, a general music class, or any other shared musical experience — can inspire children to achievement that extends far beyond their individual skill and range of expression.

The shared feeling in a large group performance sometimes defies description. Sharing an outstanding performance can be a fine aesthetic experience for the audience. The teacher who is responsible for children's music education must develop the skills needed to direct large groups of children in singing, listening, and playing classroom instruments, since large group activity often provides the most satisfying experience for the child.

PREPARING FOR LARGE GROUP ACTIVITIES

To carry out the responsibilities of the job, a wise teacher lets the students know from the beginning exactly what behavior is acceptable. Sometimes students can help set the limits for conduct. In other instances the teacher posts the rules on a chart or on the chalkboard.

State your rules in positive terms ("Be on time" rather than "Don't be late"). Set forth only the rules you intend to enforce consistently. In the two episodes that follow, there are examples of ways to prepare students for large group activities.

SPECIFIC EXAMPLES OF PREPARATION FOR LARGE GROUP ACTIVITY

EPISODE ONE

Teacher: Who remembers what we did in music class yesterday? That's right, we made up some rules that will help us work better together. Janice, please read them aloud from the chalkboard. Does everyone understand the rules? Who can tell us why it's important for everyone to follow them? Show that you understand the rule about holding your books. Open your books to page 9.

Questions for Analysis

1. Who made up the rules? Who should make them up? Why were they made up?
2. Why is the manner of holding books included in the rules?
3. Is it necessary to have rules of conduct for large group activity? Why or why not?
4. What is the role of conformity in large group activities?

EPISODE TWO

Teacher: Tomorrow, Mr. Smith is going to lead us in an assembly sing-along. I'm counting on each of you to be on your best behavior. Listen carefully to Mr. Smith's directions and sing with your very best voices. Is there anything else we should remember so that we'll be the best class in the assembly? Now open your books to page 12.

1. Who made up the rules of conduct? Who should make them up?
2. Is it necessary to remind the students of the kind of behavior expected? Why or why not?
3. Are there other ways of reviewing what is expected of the students? What are they?
4. What is the place of conformity in the assembly room?
5. How did the teacher provide for a feeling of group pride? Are there other ways?

MANAGING THE WORK PERIOD

During the work period, directions should be stated one at a time, in clear, brief language. All students must know what the teacher expects them to do. The two episodes that follow illustrate ways to manage the work period when conducting large group activities.

EPISODE ONE

<u>Teacher:</u> Open your books to page 55. Sit up tall and watch me so that we can all start together. Everyone sing "ah" like this. Try to blend your voices to sound as if one person is singing. That's better! Now hold your books up, and let's try the song on page 55. Watch those final consonants! Let's keep together as we sing them. Try to sing the sixteenth notes evenly. Back row, I need everyone's attention. Mary, Peter, José, thank you for watching so well.

Questions for Analysis

1. How did the students know what to do?
2. Were the directions clear?
3. Are there other ways of giving directions? Explain.
4. Why is it important for students to watch the teacher?

EPISODE TWO

<u>Teacher:</u> This song has two sections. As you listen, show that you hear the difference between them. Clap during the first section; stop clapping when you hear the second section.

Questions for Analysis

1. How did the students know what to do?
2. Were the directions clear?
3. Could the directions be given in another way? How?

EVALUATING LARGE GROUP ACTIVITY

When goals and objectives are known to the students, they are in a position to help judge results. However, most judgments about the musical performance will be made by the teacher. Evaluation is discussed more fully in Chapter 10. The following episodes illustrate several ways to evaluate large group activities.

SPECIFIC EXAMPLES OF EVALUATING LARGE GROUP ACTIVITY

EPISODE ONE

<u>Teacher:</u> Just before the fire drill, we taped the song on page 57. Do you remember why we taped it? Where did we decide to breathe? Let's listen to the tape and see how we did. Do you think our phrasing is getting better? Let's try the song one last time and concentrate on carrying through phrase 3. Good!

Questions for Analysis

1. What tool was used for evaluation? What other tools could be used? What are the advantages and disadvantages of each?
2. Was everyone involved in the evaluation? Should they be? Why or why not?

EPISODE TWO

<u>Teacher:</u> Who remembers one of the goals we set for ourselves for today? Do you think we reached it? Do you remember another one? Did we improve? There was one more, wasn't there? What do we need more work on?

Questions for Analysis

1. What criteria were used for evaluation?
2. How did the students know what the goals were? Was it important for them to know? Why or why not?
3. Should the evaluation be done by the group or by the teacher? Why?
4. Who finally decides whether the goal has been reached? Is this desirable? Why or why not?

The following plan illustrates how a teacher can prepare a second- or third-grade class for large group participation, manage the work period, and evaluate results.

Materials   "Wake, Snake" (page 105)
Rhythm instruments that are played by ringing, striking, or shaking

Concept   Music may have moments of silence. The musical symbols for silence are called rests.

Objectives
1. Observe rests in a song.
2. Identify rests in standard notation.
3. Create rhythm patterns in place of the rests.

Procedure
- You came into the room very nicely. Do you remember the other two rules we are working on? Yes, Della, that is correct. Did everyone hear Della?
- We are going to have a chance to practice those two rules about watching the teacher and playing instruments only when given the signal.
- Watch very closely as I sing, because I am going to be doing something with my arms. When you can, do it with me.

Sing "Wake, Snake" unaccompanied. During the rests, place your hand over your mouth as though stifling a yawn on the first beat. Stretch upward on the second beat.

WAKE, SNAKE   TRADITIONAL

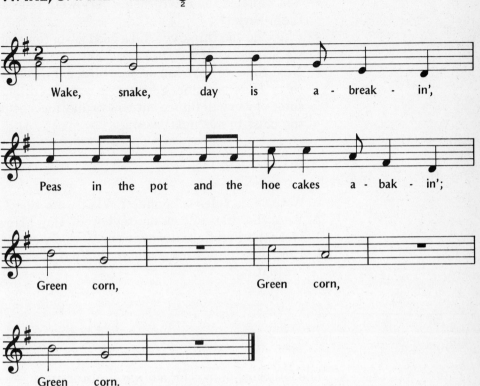

Wake, snake, day is a - break - in',

Peas in the pot and the hoe cakes a - bak - in';

Green corn,   Green corn,

Green corn.

- Good. Nearly everyone seemed to be waking up with a yawn and a stretch. This time we are going to do the same thing, only stretch in a different way. Do you ever stretch with one arm, with both arms out to the sides, or backward? Ready.
- Good. Everybody got it! What happened to my singing as you stretched? (It stopped.)
- The musical term for a silence like that is *rest*. Open your books. Find the rests in "Wake, Snake." Look this way when you have found the rests. How would you describe this rest?

- Yes, it seems to hang down from the fourth line.
- Does anyone know what kind of rest this is? (Whole rest)
- Listen to this recording of the song. What happens during the rests? (The bass plays a little tune.)
- We are going to listen again. This time you may clap your own pattern along with the bass.
- Robert, Billy, and Celeste, go to the instrument table and choose an instrument that rings. Remember our rule about waiting for my signal to play.

Following the same procedure, have a few students select instruments they can play by striking; have other students select instruments they can play by shaking. Divide the class into three groups. Have a few students in each group play instruments while others clap their patterns. Students should take turns playing the instruments.

- You handled the instruments very well. Let's see how well you can put them back.
- Class, do you think you did a good job of remembering the two rules that we are working on?
- Next time we have music, we will see if we can use our bells to fill in the rests. Here is a clue. Sometimes rests are filled in with an echo. Maybe some of you will figure out how to play an echo part and be ready to show the class in our next lesson.

Questions for Analysis

1. Were there rules of conduct? What were they?
2. Were the rules of conduct reviewed? How? How many times?
3. Were the directions always clear? Could you state them more succinctly?
4. How was the lesson evaluated? What were the criteria? Who did the evaluating?

The following plan is for a large group activity — a chorus rehearsal — and illustrates the roles of teacher and students in preparation, work period, and evaluation.

Materials
"Hallelujah" (page 107)
"Dona Nobis Pacem"
"Waters Ripple and Flow" (page 83)
Chart showing the order of songs with page numbers
Record player

Concept
Some music can be performed in more than one texture but may sound better in one than in another.

Objectives
1. Perform a piece in two textures.
2. Identify the texture of each performance.
3. Record three songs for evaluation in the next class session.

Procedure
- Lisa, will you read our objectives for today? They are posted in the usual place.
- Are there any questions?
- Open your books to the first song listed on the chart.
- Study the song "Hallelujah." We are going to make a list of everything we can find out about the song by studying the music.

HALLELUJAH FOLK ROUND FROM ISRAEL

Hal - le - lu - jah, ___ hal - le - lu - jah, ___ hal - le - lu - jah, hal - le - lu - jah. Hal - le - lu - jah, hal - le - lu - jah. ___ Hal - le - lu, hal - le - lu, hal - le - lu - jah. ___

Depending on the background of the group, a fifth- and sixth-grade chorus might be able to list these characteristics of the song.

1. Uses only one word
2. Is a round
3. Melody starts low, moves high, stays mostly high until the end
4. Has repeated rhythm patterns
5. Is in $\frac{6}{8}$ meter
6. Has three sections
7. Is a song from Israel
8. Is in minor mode

- We are going to check those observations by listening to the song. Row one, listen especially for the first two items on the list. Row two, listen for the third and fourth items, and so on.
- Row four, did the music sound as we thought it would from looking at the notation? (Yes) Explain.

Check each row. Have students listen again if there is disagreement. It may be necessary to clarify some points, such as minor or major.

- Listen again to find out how many times the song is sung. (Once)
- If we were to sing it as a three-part round, what would be the correct name for that kind of performance? (Polyphonic)
- You are ready to sing the song right now as a monophonic piece. How will you sing it? (Sing the melody alone)
- Good. Ready, sing.
- We will tape the song the way we have just sung it. When we learn to sing it as a three-part round, we will try to come to an agreement on which way most of you like it best so we can perform it that way in the concert next month. Be sure to watch.
- Ready, sing.
- I think we made a good tape of that. We will listen to it in our next rehearsal.

- Turn to the next song listed on the chart. We will tape this song first as a monophonic piece and then as a polyphonic piece. There will be no stop between. You will get your signals by watching me. Ready, sing.
- Good! You watched especially well and stayed together perfectly!
- "Waters Ripple and Flow" is next. Are you ready to tape this? Remember to start softly so that we can sing the last verse louder than the other two.
- Good. You remembered nearly everything we talked about in the last two sessions.
- Look at the objectives that Lisa read at the beginning of the period. How do you feel about our progress?
- What do we need to work on?
- We are going to have the best program we've ever had!

Questions for Analysis

1. Were the objectives for the day's lesson clear to the class? To what extent were they achieved? Are there other ways to clarify objectives for the lesson? How?
2. Were the directions always clear? What was the purpose of the chart? Do you think it helped clarify directions? Why or why not?
3. Who did most of the evaluating? What role will the students play in future evaluations?

GENERALIZATIONS

The following generalizations may be drawn from the discussion of large group activity.

Teacher's role	With few exceptions, the teacher leads the activity and directs students' thoughts and actions toward specific goals.
Students' role	All students are expected to cooperate with the teacher.
Seating	The large group is seated so that everyone is able to see and hear the teacher.
Directions	The teacher gives clear directions.
Communication	Most communication is teacher to student or student to teacher.
Decision making	The group shares in making some types of decisions, but decisions having to do with performance are usually made by the teacher.
Resolving conflicts	The teacher assumes responsibility for resolving conflicts, usually by insisting on conformity.
Goals	All members of the group accept the group goals and work toward them.
Attitude	Cohesiveness and a feeling of pride in "our" group are noticeable.
Evaluation	The group shares in making some types of evaluation, but judgments having to do with performance are made by the teacher.

SMALL GROUP ACTIVITY

Small group activities have been part of the educational program in reading and other subjects for many years, but they have not been used extensively in the music program. One reason for this, of course, is the problem of too much sound, which is unavoidable when several groups in the room are working simultaneously with different music. This becomes insignificant, though, when one considers that if the whole class always studies the same music in the same way for the same length of time, one very important aspect of the educational process is being disregarded — allowing for individual differences. When children from special education classes are included in the regular music classes, caring for individual differences is essential.

Some teachers have had great success in assigning groups of three to eight children to work quietly in various places in the room or in the hall. These small groups work independently on such assignments as planning an accompaniment (or a new interpretation) or a dance for a familiar song, practicing a difficult bell part, composing a piece for percussion instruments, or learning a song from a recording. In small group activity, students direct the work, make decisions, and resolve any conflicts that arise. The teacher acts as a guide or consultant.

PURPOSE OF SMALL GROUP ACTIVITY

Except for the very young, small group activity can be a means of musical involvement that is compatible with individual rates, levels, and styles of learning. Small group activity permits children to work at their own pace, to have a voice in making musical judgments and decisions, and to think creatively. Through small group activity, students learn to respect one another's musical efforts and ideas, to resolve their own conflicts, and to seek out sources of information. If today's students are to be fully involved and are to maintain their natural enthusiasm for music, it is essential that teachers learn to guide small group activities.

PREPARING FOR SMALL GROUP ACTIVITIES

Adequate preparation for small group activity is critical to success. When students work together in a large group, the teacher is on hand and watches the whole group to be sure that each individual understands and knows what is expected. In large group activity the teacher can clarify directions or restate a problem immediately. In small group activity the musical preparation must be thorough so that participants have the background necessary to work independently. Some teachers begin with only one small group, choosing children who are mature enough to work together without constant supervision and assigning those children to an available space in the room, such as the "library" table or just outside the door in the hall. To conduct small group activity successfully, the teacher must be sure that the students have the musical background necessary to complete the task, are mature enough to work without close supervision, and are given directions they fully understand.

EPISODE ONE

<u>Teacher:</u> That was very good! You sang the loud phrases beautifully, and no one forgot to stop singing on the soft phrases! Jane, June, Robert, Phillip, and Lisa, please go to the table in the back of the room and plan a percussion composition that has both loud and soft sections. Plan your composition for drum, triangle, tambourine, sticks, and tone block. You know how the instruments sound, so you shouldn't have to play them. When you're ready, come back to your desks.

Questions for Analysis

1. Did the children know the difference between loud and soft? How did the teacher know? Is this a good way to tell? Are there other ways?
2. Was it important for the children to know the difference between loud and soft? Why or why not?
3. Had the children had previous experience with percussion instruments? Was it necessary? Why or why not?
4. How was the group chosen? Are there other ways?
5. Where did the group work? Could they have worked elsewhere?
6. What was the group supposed to do when the assignment was finished? Was this direction necessary? Why or why not?

EPISODE TWO

<u>Teacher:</u> Sing "Row, Row, Row Your Boat." Good! Yesterday, we decided that this song has three different rhythm patterns. Who can clap one of them? Which words in the song fit that rhythm pattern? Who can clap another rhythm pattern? What does the third one sound like? I have a special assignment for seven people who know how to work together. Hal, please read it from the chalkboard.

<u>Hal</u> (*reading from the chalkboard*):

1. Choose three different-sounding percussion instruments (two of each) from the instrument box and go out into the hall.
2. Working together, use the three rhythm patterns in "Row, Row, Row Your Boat" to put together a composition for percussion instruments.
3. Use each rhythm pattern at least one time; don't use any pattern more than three times.
4. Decide on the order of the rhythm patterns and write it down.
5. Assign one kind of percussion instrument to each pattern.
6. Choose a conductor and decide who will play each instrument.
7. Practice your composition.
8. Return to the room and perform it for the class.

Teacher: Thank you, Hal. Does everyone understand the assignment? What should the group do if they can't agree on how many times to use each rhythm pattern or if they have trouble assigning percussion instruments? If they don't agree on one of the rhythm patterns, where can they check it? If someone doesn't cooperate, what should the group do? Now, who would like to work on this assignment? All right, Denise, John, Kathy, Mary, Betty, Tom, and Hal.

Questions for Analysis

1. Did the children know the song? Did they need to?
2. Did the children know the rhythm patterns? Did they need to?
3. How else could the teacher have determined whether the class knew the three rhythm patterns?
4. How many small groups were there? How were they selected?
5. How were directions given? How else could they have been given?
6. What provision was made for resolution of conflict?
7. What provision was made to avoid useless arguing of facts?
8. Was a leader appointed? Should one have been? Why or why not?

REVIEW AND ASSIGNMENT IN SMALL GROUP ACTIVITY

Children working in small groups usually need to review and clarify the musical learning they will be dealing with. The following episodes illustrate some approaches.

SPECIFIC EXAMPLES OF REVIEW AND ASSIGNMENT IN SMALL GROUP ACTIVITY

EPISODE ONE

Teacher: Very good! I like the way you remembered to slow down the middle part of "Play for Ma Dogoma." For today, everybody stay at your regular places to work. The people at each table will make up a sound piece that has one fast part and one slow part. John, Jack, Mary, and Tom, your tables will make up pieces for hand sounds. Who remembers what hand sounds are? Lisa, David, and Jan, your groups will make up pieces for vocal sounds — remember, vocal sounds are any sounds that you can make with your voice. Are there any questions? When I flick the lights, your time is up.

Questions for Analysis

1. Did the children know the difference between fast and slow? How did the teacher know? Was this a good way to tell? Are there other ways?
2. Was it necessary for the children to know the difference between fast and slow? Why or why not?
3. Had the children had previous experience with hand sounds? With vocal sounds?
4. How were the children grouped? Was this a good way? Why or why not?

5. How was the assignment given? What made it clear or unclear?
6. What was the signal for stopping? Are there others that might be more effective?
7. Is it necessary for a teacher to give a signal for stopping?

EPISODE TWO

Teacher: Sing "Hill an' Gully." Do you remember it? Good! Let's sing it again, and this time watch my conducting very carefully to see if you can tell when I want you to sing loud and when I want you to sing soft. That was pretty good! How did you know when to sing loud? How did you know when to sing soft? The first person in each row, please stand and go to one of the charts posted on the wall. All the charts say the same thing. Denise, please tell us what your chart says.

Denise (*reading from the chart*):
1. Open your book to "Poor Wayfaring Stranger."
2. Decide which part of "Poor Wayfaring Stranger" you think should be loud.
3. Decide which part of "Poor Wayfaring Stranger" you think should be soft.
4. Choose a conductor to practice conducting the "louds" and "softs" while you sing.
5. Your conductor will lead the class in singing "Poor Wayfaring Stranger" your way.

Teacher: Are there any questions? The people at the charts are leaders. When I call your row, please stand and join your leader at the chart. What will you do if your group can't agree? What will you do if someone doesn't cooperate? When I raise my hand, your time is up.

Questions for Analysis

1. What work was done prior to the small group work? Was it necessary? Why or why not?
2. How did the teacher indicate when the children should sing loud and when they should sing soft? Was this a good way to indicate it? Is there a better way?
3. How were the group leaders chosen? How else could they have been chosen?
4. How were the directions for the group work given? In what other ways could they have been given?
5. How were students assigned to groups? Was this a good idea? Why or why not?
6. What reminders were given for working in groups? Why were the reminders given?
7. What was the signal for stopping? Is this a good signal? Why or why not?

MANAGING THE WORK PERIOD AND REPORTING IN SMALL GROUP ACTIVITY

Even a mature, self-disciplined group can become so involved and excited about their small group assignment that they are unmindful of the amount of sound they are generating. You must make it very clear exactly what signal will be used to call for the attention of all the groups and then consistently (and insistently) adhere to it.

SPECIFIC EXAMPLES OF MANAGING THE WORK PERIOD
AND REPORTING IN SMALL GROUP ACTIVITY

EPISODE ONE

Teacher: Thank you for stopping on signal. Jan says her group can't hear one another. What do the rest of you have to do? Lisa, is your group ready? Please tell us what your assignment was.

Questions for Analysis

1. Why did the teacher stop the class?
2. How else could the children have been made aware of the problem?
3. Who solved the problem?
4. Why did the teacher ask Lisa what her assignment was?

EPISODE TWO

Teacher: Denise, did you raise your hand for help? How can your group come to an agreement? Does everyone understand the point Tom is making? I think we'll tape our reports today. Is any group ready? Is there any group that hasn't reported? Everyone please come back to your desks.

Questions for Analysis

1. Describe some ways of rearranging the room to accommodate small group work.
2. Who solved the problem that Denise's group had? What was the role of the teacher in resolving the conflict?
3. What procedure was used for reporting to the class? Why?
4. How would you describe the role of the teacher? How would you describe the role of the students?

EVALUATING SMALL GROUP ACTIVITY

Evaluating small group work can be critical to its success. Children can be very self-conscious about performing for their peers. Even a hint of ridicule can turn the performance and the evaluation of small group work into a devastating experience. The teacher sets a good climate for evaluation, making clear the criteria to be used. These criteria should relate directly to the assigned task — "Was the assignment fulfilled?" not "Was the product good or bad?" If behavior is to be evaluated, the criteria for acceptable behavior must be made clear. The climate in a classroom improves when behavior is evaluated in positive ways, sometimes even to the extent of ignoring inappropriate behavior.

The following episodes illustrate some techniques for evaluating small group work.

EPISODE ONE

<u>Teacher</u>: What was the assignment for your group, Bob? Does everyone agree that Bob's group followed the assignment? Which part came first, the fast one or the slow one? Was there more than one fast part? Was there more than one slow part? Does any group have a different arrangement of fast and slow parts?

Questions for Analysis

1. Why was the assignment reviewed?
2. What was the criterion for evaluation?
3. Was a value judgment required? Did the teacher indicate that there should be a value judgment?
4. Should a value judgment have been made? If so, by whom? When? If not, why not?

EPISODE TWO

<u>Teacher</u>: What are some good things about the way we worked today? Where do we need to improve? Are there any questions about the assignment? On Friday, we'll listen to the rest of the tapes and decide what to work on next. In the meantime, see if you can find time to practice some of the things we've learned today.

Questions for Analysis

1. What did the teacher ask the students to evaluate? Was this a good idea? Are there other ways to evaluate?
2. What provision was made for the next lesson? Was this good? Why or why not?
3. How were students encouraged to do out-of-school work?

The following plan illustrates one way a teacher may prepare a fourth- or fifth-grade class for small group work, provide for review and give the assignment, manage the work period and evaluate the work.

Materials Rhythm instruments
Melody instruments
Autoharps
"Old Blue" (page 36)
"Don Gato" (page 115)
Record player
Recordings of excerpts from Beethoven: *Symphony No. 6,* "Allegro"; Honegger: *Pacific 231*; Dukas: *The Sorcerer's Apprentice*

Concept In some music a variety of tone colors is used to help paint a picture or tell a story.

Objectives
1. Create sound effects that help tell the story of Don Gato.
2. Use sound effects to help tell a story or paint a picture in an original composition.

- Open your books to "Old Blue." What kind of song is "Old Blue"? (A ballad)
- What is a ballad? (A song that tells a story)
- As we sing the song, remember that we are telling a story and don't let your tongue and lips get lazy. Ready, sing.
- That was good. I could understand every word.
- Look at "Don Gato." This is a folk song from Mexico. We are going to read the words of the song out loud and find answers for the questions listed on the chart.

DON GATO
FOLK SONG FROM MEXICO   ENGLISH WORDS BY MARGARET MARKS

1. Oh, Se - ñor Don Ga - to was a cat,___
2. "I a - dore you!" wrote the la - dy cat,___

On a high, red roof Don Ga - to sat.___
Who was fluff - y, white, and nice and fat.___

He went there to read a let - ter, meow, meow, meow,
There was not a sweet - er kit - ty,

Where the read - ing light was bet - ter, meow, meow, meow,
In the coun - try or the cit - y,

'Twas a love note for Don Ga - to!___
And she said she'd wed Don Ga - to!___

3. Oh, Don Gato jumped so happily
He fell off the roof and broke his knee,
Broke his ribs and all his whiskers, . . .
And his little solar plexus, . . .
"¡Ay carramba!" cried Don Gato!

4. Then the doctors all came on the run
Just to see if something could be done,
And they held a consultation, . . .
About how to save their patient, . . .
How to save Señor Don Gato!

(Continued)

5. But in spite of everything they tried
Poor Señor Don Gato up and died,
Oh, it wasn't very merry, . . .
Going to the cemetery, . . .
For the ending of Don Gato!

6. When the funeral passed the market square
Such a smell of fish was in the air,
Though his burial was slated, . . .
He became re-animated! . . .
He came back to life, Don Gato!

- Melinda, will you read the chart, please?

  "Don Gato," Mexican folk song
  1. Is the song a ballad? How can you tell?
  2. What is the main idea?
  3. What is the order of the events?

- Thank you, Melinda. All right, class, we will read aloud together. Remember, your reading will be more expressive if you observe the punctuation. Ready, together.

Call on volunteers to answer the questions. Teach the song by rote.[1]

- Listen to the recording of the first verse.[2] Listen especially for a sound effect describing Don Gato. You will hear it at the end of phrases 1 and 2. What instrument is played? (Flute)
- Can you think of a classroom instrument you could use at the end of phrases 1 and 2 in verse 2 to describe the lady cat?
- Good. You have the idea. Nancy, read the chart for directions.

  1. Work in a group with a leader.
  2. Use melody instruments, rhythm instruments, and vocal sounds.
  3. Make sound effects as follows:
     Andy's group: "Don Gato jumped so happily
     . . . and broke his knee"
     Billy's group: ". . . doctors all came on the run
     . . . see what could be done"

- Are there any questions?
- Remember that sound effects should help tell the story. You will have five minutes. I will flick the light once as a warning; twice means give me your attention.
- Thank you for paying attention on signal. How many have finished? If your group is not ready to play, Jane, explain what you are considering and let the class help you decide.

Have each group play their sound effect as the class sings. Ask the class if every group played their sound effect at the correct time, and if each group used all three sound sources or fewer than three. Avoid making value judgments.

- Here are four charts with assignments. Each group may choose the assignment they would like to do.

---

[1]See Hints for Teaching Rote Songs, p. 186.

[2]The recording that accompanies *Silver Burdett Music 4*, © 1981, includes all the verses of "Don Gato." Use that recording if possible.

ASSIGNMENT 1

Create sound effects that help tell the story of all the verses of "Old Blue."

ASSIGNMENT 2

Choose a poem or nursery rhyme that tells a story or suggests sounds. Create sound effects for it. (Provide a variety of poems and nursery rhymes.)

ASSIGNMENT 3

Create sound effects that describe the photograph. (Display a large photograph or painting of a severe storm.)

ASSIGNMENT 4

Create sound effects that describe the photograph. (Display a large photograph of a football game.)

- If your group finishes before the class does, you may go to the record table and listen to the recordings. You will hear how Beethoven, Dukas, and Honegger,[3] all important composers, used music to help tell a story or paint a picture in sound. Read the information that is on the table about each composition. Then make a list of instruments you recognize in the order that you hear them and a list of changes in dynamics in the order that you hear them.
- You may begin your work.
- Thank you for stopping on signal. We will have to continue our group work at the next lesson. Please put all instruments in their proper places.

Questions for Analysis

1. What did the teacher do to prepare for small group work? Was anything omitted? What?
2. How were groups assigned? Are there other ways?
3. How were the directions clarified? Are there other ways? What are some of them?
4. What reminders did the teacher give the class about small group work? Were some omitted? What were they?
5. How was the small group work evaluated? What were the criteria?

The following plan is for an upper level class that has been playing recorder for several months. In what ways does this plan serve the purpose of small group activity as stated on page 109?

Materials "Dayenu" (page 118)
Recorders
Autoharps (at least two; six or seven would be better)
Finger cymbals
Tambourines
High drum and low drum

Concepts Some music has two different sections. This is usually designated as AB form. The beat sometimes changes tempo (rate of speed) within a piece.

Objective Demonstrate recognition of AB form and change of tempo within one piece by responding appropriately through movement and by playing instruments appropriately.

---

[3]See Materials for this lesson, p. 114.

Procedure
- Listen to this song. What part of the world do you think it comes from? (Probably from the Middle East)
- Why do you think so? (The words suggest this, and after the title you see the words *Hebrew Passover Song*.)

DAYENU   HEBREW PASSOVER SONG   ENGLISH WORDS BY ELIZABETH S. BACHMAN

1. He has led us out of E - gypt, led His peo - ple out of E - gypt,
He has led us out of E - gypt, *da - ye - nu.*

REFRAIN
Da - da - ye - nu,_____ da - da - ye - nu,_____
Da - da - ye - nu, da - ye - nu da - ye - nu da - ye - nu,
Da - da - ye - nu,_____ da - da - ye - nu,_____
Da - da - ye - nu, da - ye - nu da - ye - nu.

2. He has given us the Sabbath, given us the holy Sabbath,
He has given us the Sabbath, *dayenu. Refrain*

3. He has given us the Torah, given us the blessed Torah,
He has given us the Torah, *dayenu. Refrain*

- Look at the song in your books. Study the notation as you listen. Are the phrases all the same length? (No)
- What happens to the tempo in section B? (It gets faster.)
- Listen again and tap the steady beat with your toe.
- This time, stand and mark time in place while you listen.
- Jay, will you come to the chalkboard and mark the steady beats? Everyone else continue to mark time in place. Listen for the place where the music changes tempo.

- Good. Be seated and sing the whole song. Ready, sing.
- Last week we learned the polka step. You remember saying to yourself, "step, together, step, hop." Since we have very little space in this room, please stand and do the polka step in place. Say "step, together, step, hop."
- We will work in groups today. You may choose your group. Decide which assignment you would prefer to work on. Joan, will you read what is posted above station 1?

STATION 1 – RECORDER PLAYERS

1. Practice this simplified recorder part. It fits with section A of "Dayenu" when played on the steady beat.

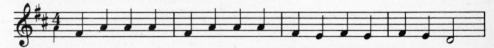

2. When you think you can play it correctly, ask the teacher to check your playing.
3. Practice section B as it is written in the book. Remember that section B gets faster toward the end.

- Peter, will you read what is to be done at station 2?

STATION 2 – RHYTHM INSTRUMENT PLAYERS

1. Two people practice playing the steady beat on the tambourine. Play section A of "Dayenu" only. Use this pattern:

hit   shake   hit   shake

2. Four people practice playing finger cymbals in section B only. Play the rhythm of the words.
3. One person plays the low drum part in section B only.

Low  etc.

4. One person plays the high drum part in section B only.

High  etc.

- Linda, read what is to be done at station 3.

STATION 3 – AUTOHARP PLAYERS

1. Practice playing the D and A₇ chords as marked in the "Dayenu."
2. Three people play the beat, using picks.
3. Three people hold three mallets each between the fingers of the strumming hand and brush the mallets over the strings in the rhythm of the melody. Brush back and forth, using all the strings.

- Mina, will you read instructions for station 4?

STATION 4 – DANCERS

1. Study the directions below and practice the dance.
2. Then listen to the recording of "Dayenu." Practice the dance with the music and decide what you will do during the interludes.

FORMATION: ANY NUMBER OF DANCERS STAND IN A CIRCLE (FACING THE CENTER) HOLDING JOINED HANDS AT SHOULDER LEVEL.

Section A (short phrases of 4 beats)

4 BEATS:	STEP SIDEWAYS RIGHT, STEP LEFT IN BACK OF RIGHT, STEP RIGHT, STAMP LEFT.
4 BEATS:	STEP SIDEWAYS LEFT, STEP RIGHT IN BACK OF LEFT, STEP LEFT, STAMP RIGHT.
4 BEATS:	STEP FORWARD RIGHT, STAMP LEFT WHILE RAISING ARMS. STEP BACKWARD LEFT, STAMP RIGHT, LOWERING ARMS.
4 BEATS:	STAMP RIGHT, LEFT, RIGHT, HOLD.

Section B (long phrases of 16 beats)

16 BEATS:	WITH HANDS STILL JOINED, ALL TURN SLIGHTLY TO THE RIGHT AND DANCE 7 POLKA STEPS TO THE RIGHT, STARTING WITH RIGHT FOOT.
	TO COMPLETE THE PHRASE, DROP HANDS, TURN AROUND TO THE RIGHT, AND QUICKLY JOIN HANDS AGAIN, THE CIRCLE IS NOW INSIDE OUT.
16 BEATS:	DANCE 7 POLKA STEPS TO THE RIGHT, STARTING WITH THE RIGHT FOOT. TO COMPLETE THE PHRASE, DROP HANDS AND TURN RIGHT. THE CIRCLE IS NOW FACING CENTER AGAIN.

- Are there any questions?
- You may now choose a station to work at. If there are more than eight people at the station, please go to the station of your second choice. Remember the signal for paying attention. What is it, again?
- Good. Take your places.
- Thank you for paying attention on signal. We will continue work at the next lesson. If you would like to check out an instrument to take home to practice, see me at noon. Please put your instruments away before you leave. Class dismissed.

Questions for Analysis

1. What did students have to know to complete the work at the stations?
2. Did the activities provide for different levels of skill? Different interests? Different modes of learning?
3. What space was needed for these activities?
4. What materials were required?
5. Was there an evaluation? Why or why not?

GENERALIZATIONS

The following generalizations may be drawn from the discussion of small group activity.

Teacher's role   The teacher initiates idea exchange and cooperation and shares in problem solving. Sometimes the teacher plays the role of a member of the group to provide for student- or group-initiated activities.

Students' role	Students share the leadership role with the teacher; they are free to express disagreement with the teacher's proposals. All students cooperate and participate in the activities.
Seating	Students are seated so that they are face to face.
Communication	There is student-to-student as well as teacher-to-student communication.
Decision making	The group shares in decision making.
Resolving conflicts	The group resolves its own conflicts and does not require policing by the teacher. Consensus is arrived at by means of discussion, and each member's opinion is respected.
Goals	Goals of the group are accepted by all the group's members.
Attitude	There is cohesiveness within the group and a feeling of pride in "our" effort.
Evaluation	The group is responsible for its own evaluation. The teacher identifies areas of weakness in understanding and skill development and incorporates them in future plans.

ASSESSMENT 1 Contrast the teacher's role in large group work with that in small group activities. Give examples of different ways the teacher (a) prepares for large group work, (b) manages the available time, and (c) evaluates student achievement.

ASSESSMENT 2 Study the following episodes. Decide whether each is an example of a large group activity or a small group activity. Determine which generalization(s) applies to each episode. Explain your answers.

EPISODE ONE

<u>Teacher:</u> I'm going to play a recording of a song you know. Listen carefully and see if you can tell whether the form of the song is AB or ABA. John, why do you think the form is ABA? What are the words of section A? Let's listen again, and this time make any motion you like when you hear section B. Very good! Everybody stand and let's sing the song.

EPISODE TWO

<u>Teacher:</u> Did you have any problems as you worked in your groups today? Jane? Why do you think your group couldn't agree, Jane? Did everyone in your group have a chance to share his or her ideas? Can anyone suggest how Jane's group can work better together?

EPISODE THREE

<u>Teacher:</u> I have some wonderful news for you this morning. Our class has been invited to sing in the assembly program at the end of the month. We'll only be singing one song, so let's make it something very special, something that you really like. Does anyone have any suggestions? Kathy, please list the suggestions on the board. Tom? Betty? Shirley? Harry? Anyone else? Let's take a vote to decide which song we'll sing.

EPISODE FOUR

Now that we've chosen to sing "Angelique-O" in the assembly program, we have to decide how we want to "dress up" our song. Shall we have an Autoharp accompaniment or a piano accompaniment? Nancy, since you play the Autoharp so well, choose three people and teach them the Autoharp chords for "Angelique-O." You may practice in the hall. Now, I'd like all the people in row one to work together to make up a percussion accompaniment for the song. Rows three, five, and seven, you work on percussion accompaniments, too. Rows two, four, and six, I'd like each of you to make up a dance or a pantomime for the song. Each row, choose a leader and get right to work. You may have the whole period. Tomorrow we'll decide which percussion accompaniment or dance works best.

EPISODE FIVE

Teacher: Look at the chart on the easel. Raise your hand if you can name one of the colors that you see. Tommy? Billy? Anne? I have a brand new song for you today. It's all about a girl named Jennie Jenkins. Jennie has lots of different-colored dresses to wear. Listen to the song very carefully. Does Jennie have a dress for every color on the chart? Barbara? Very good! Let's all listen once more. As soon as you can, try humming with the recording.

ASSESSMENT 3   Study the song "Sakura." Devise a plan for teaching it to a large group.

Extend your plan to show how you would care for individual differences by grouping. The following resources are available.

1. A recording of "Sakura" with a koto accompaniment (record 2)
2. A recording of Eto: *Variations on Sakura* played on the koto (record 2)
3. Recorders and a recorder part
4. Directions for a dance

The following is a guide for listening to the recording of Eto: *Variations on Sakura*.

Theme (melody)
Played with countermelody
Countermelody sometimes uses contrasting rhythm pattern
Ends with a downward glissando

Variation 1
Theme in low register; countermelody in high register
Faster tempo
Many short sounds
Ends with a downward glissando

Variation 2
Theme and countermelody seem to come together and separate
Slower tempo
Ends with high short sounds
No glissando at end

Variation 3
Countermelody elaborate — many short sounds
Fast tempo
Many repeated tones moving mostly downward

You may wish to give the class some background information about the music of Japan and the role of dance. Explain that the movements for "Sakura" help to tell of the beauty of the cherry tree. Each movement is done first to the right and then to the left, filling one phrase of music.

Have students stand in any formation. For the beginning pose, the right hand should rest on top of the left hand at waist level, with both palms up. After each pose in the dance, the hands should return to the beginning pose. The eyes should follow arm movements in each pose.

⌒

Sakura,

NOD HEAD
TO RIGHT.

Sakura,

NOD HEAD
TO LEFT.

⌒

Cherry blossoms

RAISE RIGHT ARM
OVERHEAD, KEEPING
LEFT HAND IN
BEGINNING POSE.

ev'rywhere,

RAISE LEFT ARM
OVERHEAD, KEEPING
RIGHT HAND IN
BEGINNING POSE.

⌒

Clouds of glory

EXTEND BOTH ARMS
SIDEWAYS TO
RIGHT.

fill the sky,

EXTEND BOTH
ARMS SIDEWAYS
TO LEFT.

⌒

Mist of beauty

TOUCH THIGHS WITH
BOTH HANDS. EXTEND
BOTH ARMS SIDEWAYS
TO RIGHT.

in the air,

TOUCH THIGHS WITH
BOTH HANDS. EXTEND
BOTH ARMS SIDEWAYS
TO LEFT.

⌒

Lovely colors

PRETEND TO SPREAD
RIGHT KIMONO
SLEEVE IN FRONT
AND LOOK TOWARD
RIGHT.

floating by,

PRETEND TO
SPREAD LEFT
KIMONO SLEEVE
IN FRONT AND
LOOK TOWARD
LEFT.

⌒

Sakura,

RAISE BOTH ARMS,
RIGHT ARM HIGHER
THAN LEFT.

Sakura,

RAISE BOTH ARMS,
LEFT ARM HIGHER
THAN RIGHT.

⌒

Let all

BEND RIGHT ARM,
HAND POINTING UP.
PLACE LEFT HAND
UNDER RIGHT ELBOW.
LOOK TOWARD
RIGHT.

come singing.

BEND LEFT ARM,
HAND POINTING
UP. PLACE
RIGHT HAND
UNDER LEFT
ELBOW. LOOK
TOWARD LEFT.

7 *Individualizing Instruction*

CHAPTER OBJECTIVE | *Write a plan that will provide for individual differences among children. Illustrate two of the following:*

(a) *traditional teaching methods,*

(b) *learning contracts,*

(c) *individualized learning packets,*

(d) *grouping.*

When you as teacher stand before your class, you cannot have the attitude that your function is merely to dispense information or to guide an activity. You cannot expect that all your students will absorb information or participate in activities with the same eagerness, quickness, and understanding. Such an assumption would deny the existence of students' individual personalities, capabilities, and needs. When you plan lessons, you must be aware of the individuality of your students and take care to provide for it.

Providing for individual differences is especially important when children from special education groups are included in your classes.[1] You should confer with the special education teacher to be fully aware of children's different levels of ability and different rates and styles of learning. A good rule of thumb is to plan for three factors: a range of ability levels; a range of rates of mastery — fast and slow; and a variety of response modes — visual, auditory, and kinesthetic-tactile.

TRADITIONAL WAYS OF PROVIDING FOR INDIVIDUAL DIFFERENCES

There are many ways in which you can provide for the individual differences among your students. Some of them are amazingly simple. For example, you individualize instruction when you rephrase a question or

---

[1]For more information, see the section on "Music Education for Exceptional Children" in the Bibliography.

clarify a direction for the students who raise their hands to indicate that they do not understand. You individualize instruction when you decide to ask John to improvise a drum accompaniment, because while John has difficulty controlling his singing voice, he can play an exciting bongo drum part.

You individualize instruction when you recognize Mary's ability to play the Autoharp and let her teach some of her classmates the chords for a new song. You can individualize instruction by extending a deadline so that the student who "takes a little longer" can complete the assignment, or by agreeing to accept the work that a student has been able to finish in a given period of time even if it is not the complete assignment. You individualize instruction when you write out directions for those who have poor retention. All these acts show that you care about your students as individuals, and yet they require no more than thought and careful planning on the teacher's part.

SPECIFIC EXAMPLES OF TRADITIONAL METHODS

The following episodes are examples of simple ways in which a teacher can individualize instruction. Study the episodes and then answer the Questions for Analysis.

EPISODE ONE

Teacher: Next Wednesday your parents will be visiting our classroom. Suppose we put on a special talent show for them during our music period. John, you played the recorder part on "Dayenu" so well yesterday. Would you play it again when we sing the song next week? Remember the song Jane sang for us this morning, the one her sister taught her? Let's ask her to sing it next Wednesday, and maybe before then she'll teach us the chorus so that we can all join in. Angelo, will you play the drum on "Clap Your Hands" next week? You may take the drum home to practice if you like.

Questions for Analysis

1. How did the teacher indicate a knowledge of the students' abilities?
2. Was every child given the same assignment?

EPISODE TWO

Teacher: That was very good. I can tell that you really like to sing "Dayenu." Let's add a different kind of accompaniment to the song. There are three guitars on the table in the front of the room. Is there anyone who can take a guitar and play just the D chord every time it occurs in the song? All right, Pearl. Who can take the second guitar and play just the A_7 chords? Jim. On which word will you play your first A_7 chord, Jim? Who can take the third guitar and play both chords? Charles. Which chord will Charles play first? Guitarists, decide whether you will strum once or twice per measure. The rest of you, close your books and try to sing the song from memory as the guitarists play. Ready?

1. What activities were students asked to perform? Which was the most difficult?
2. How did the teacher make certain that each student knew what to do?

EPISODE THREE

<u>Teacher:</u> Paul, have you had a chance to work out the guitar chords for "Matilda"? Are you ready to play for the class yet? I understand. It's not easy to play. We'll wait until you're ready. Why don't you ask Mr. Johnson if he will help you after school. He's a fine guitarist. Marian, you're practicing the guitar chords for "Mama Don't 'Low," aren't you? Can you play the whole song yet? Then why don't you try playing just the section that you know as the class sings. Good! That's really coming along, Marian.

Questions for Analysis

1. Did the teacher set a strict deadline for completion of the individual assignment? How do you know?
2. What resource did the teacher suggest to Paul?
3. On what basis did the teacher evaluate Marian's work?

The following plan is another illustration of traditional ways in which teachers can provide for individual differences.

Materials	"Mary Had a Baby" Rhythm instruments Bells
Concepts	1. A song may have both long and short phrases. 2. A song may have repeated patterns in both melody and rhythm.
Objective	Perform and identify phrases of different lengths and repeated patterns in rhythm and melody.
Procedure	Teach the following song.

MARY HAD A BABY BLACK SPIRITUAL

SOLO · CHORUS

Mar - y had a ba - by, Yes, Lord!

ALL

The peo - ple keep a - com - in' an' the train done gone.

2. What did She name Him?

Yes, Lord!

What did She name Him?

Yes, my Lord!

What did She name Him?

Yes, Lord!

The people keep a-comin' an' the train done gone.

3. Named Him King Jesus,

4. Where was He born?

5. Born in a stable,

Ask children to listen to the first verse of the song to find out which words, or phrases, are repeated ("Mary had a baby" and "Yes, Lord"). It will probably take two listenings to discover both phrases.

Ask students to listen again for other phrases that are repeated. Divide the class into two groups. Have one group sing the solo parts and the other group the chorus parts. (You sing the last phrase.) Have the class stand, and as they sing have them stretch upward on the solo parts and come down again on the chorus parts. Have them compare the length and size of the stretches they are able to make on each of the phrases. Ask questions that will lead them to realize that there are six short phrases and one long one. Sing the entire song.

Hum the first phrase and ask children which phrase it is. (The first, third, and fifth phrases sound the same.) Demonstrate how the like phrases can be played on bells. Pantomime the motion in the air. Ask children to pantomime playing the bells with you on those phrases. When you see some children pantomime correctly, have them play the solo part on the bells as the class sings the chorus parts.

Sing and clap the first "Yes, Lord," asking the class to find it in the song. Question them until they discover that "Yes, Lord" is sung twice on the chorus parts in that rhythm and once in a different rhythm. Ask children to clap on the two "Yes, Lord" phrases that have like rhythms and snap fingers on the chorus phrase that is different: "Yes, my Lord."

- Can you suggest a rhythm instrument to play on the phrases that we clapped? (A tambourine would be good because it could sustain the half notes.)
- What would you suggest for the "Yes, my Lord" phrase where we snapped our fingers? (Drum)

- Jane, Jim, and Billy, will you play the tambourines?
- Matthew, Becky, and Dolores, will you play the drums on the "Yes, my Lord" phrase?
- We'll sing the song with bells, tambourines, drums, and wood block.
- Here on the chalkboard is a plan for singing and playing:

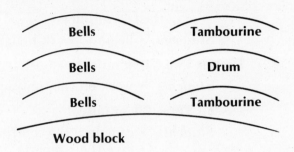

Questions for Analysis

1. What provision was made for children with a slow rate of learning?
2. Was there a range of difficulty in the tasks? What was the most difficult? What was the easiest?
3. What device was used to help children with poor retention? To help visual learners? To help kinesthetic learners?

LEARNING CONTRACTS

Learning contracts as a means of individualizing instruction have been used successfully in language arts programs for some time. Some teachers have been using learning contracts in music classes, and they, too, have experienced success. A learning contract is simply a written agreement, drawn up by the teacher and signed by the student, that obligates the student to complete a specified number of tasks. The contract may or may not set a time limit for completion of the work. Usually the contract provides options from which the student may choose. Before the student signs the contract, he or she must check off the options that will be completed.

While most of the options will require that students work alone, some may require that a small group of students work together. Once a student has signed a contract, the options agreed to must be completed and then a final report given to the teacher or to the class. The report may be in the form of a performance if, for example, the option required the learner to accompany a familiar song on the Autoharp; it may be an oral report if the option required the student to research and share the findings with the class; or it may be a written report if the option required the student to write four rhythm patterns in four meter, using only quarter notes and eighth notes.

The following outline shows how learning contracts may be introduced to a class for the first time.

Lesson One (first 20 minutes)

Teacher • introduces the concept
• clarifies the concept through activities
• presents sample contracts to the entire class
• gives each student a copy of the contract
• answers students' questions about the contract

Students • check off the options they will work on
• sign the contracts

(last 10 minutes)

Students • begin to work individually or in small groups

Lesson Two (30 minutes)

Students • work on the contracts

Lesson Three (30 minutes)

Students • complete the contracts
• give their reports

Lesson Four (30 minutes)

Students • complete their reports
• identify next steps

Teachers who use learning contracts as a means of individualizing instruction usually incorporate them into their lesson plans about 20 percent of the time.

SPECIFIC EXAMPLES OF LEARNING CONTRACTS

The following are two learning contracts for a music class. Study the contracts and then answer the Questions for Analysis.

MUSIC CONTRACT ONE

I will complete two of the following.

____ 1. I will study the words of two songs that I do not know and decide whether each of the songs should be sung fast or slow. I will give reasons for each of my decisions.

____ 2. I will study the notes of two songs that I do not know and decide whether each of the songs should be sung fast or slow. I will give reasons for each of my decisions.

____ 3. I will look up the meaning of *largo* and *allegro*. I will demonstrate the difference between them by making up a piece for percussion instruments and playing it first as though it were marked *allegro* and then as though it were marked *largo*.

____ 4. I will work with three other students to make up a percussion piece that has one fast part and one slow part. We will perform the piece.

___ 5. I will list five songs that I know and put a check mark next to the ones that I think should be sung fast.

___ 6. I will make up a dance for "Dayenu" showing the difference between the fast and slow parts of the song.

___ 7. I will sing or play one song that I know, first slowly, then fast.

Name _____ Date _____

Questions for Analysis

1. Do the options in the learning contract provide for varying levels of ability? If so, how? (Renumber the list of options in the order of their difficulty.)
2. What concept is emphasized in each option?
3. What skills do students need to perform each option?
4. What equipment do students need to perform each option?
5. With what age level would you use this contract?
6. Are provisions made for children with special needs? If so, what are they? If not, how could you provide them?

MUSIC CONTRACT TWO

I will complete three of the following.

___ 1. I will make up a piece for Autoharp that has two sections. One section will have a steady beat; the other section will have no beat.

___ 2. I will choose a percussion instrument and write a piece for it that has meter in 2.

___ 3. I will choose a percussion instrument and write a piece for it that has two sections. The first section will have beats in sets of two; the second section will have beats in sets of three.

___ 4. I will look in my music book to find each of the following:
a. Two songs with a meter signature of $\frac{2}{4}$
b. Three songs with a meter signature of $\frac{3}{4}$
c. One song with a meter signature of $\frac{4}{4}$

___ 5. I will list five sounds I hear every day that have a steady beat.

___ 6. I will list five sounds I hear every day that have no beat.

___ 7. There are five recordings on the music table. I will listen to the selections indicated on each recording to find one that has a steady beat and one that has no beat. I will play these two selections for the class.

Name _____ Date _____

1. Do the options in the learning contract provide for varying levels of ability? If so, how? (Renumber the list of options in the order of their difficulty.)
2. What concept is emphasized in each option?
3. What skills do students need to perform each option?
4. What equipment do students need to perform each option?
5. With what age level would you use this contract?
6. Is provision made for special education students? If so, how? If not, how could you provide for them?

The following plan illustrates the use of learning contracts in a third- or fourth-grade class.

Materials   "He's Got the Whole World in His Hands" (page 134)
Autoharps
Bells, bass xylophone, metallophones
Recorders

Concept   A melody sometimes outlines a chord.

Objectives   1. Identify the F chord as outlined in the song.
2. Identify chord changes marked in the accompaniment.
3. Play a harmony part.

Procedure   Teach the song by rote.[2]

- Look at the music. How many chords are used in this song?
- What are they? (F and C_7)
- Look at the chord chart. What bells are needed for the F chord? (F, A, C)
- Look at the beginning phrase of the song. What notes do you see? (C, A, F)

You may need to help children find the notes. A chart similar to the one on page 194 will help them locate letter names and relate them to the bells. Or you might ask students to give the letter name of the first note (C). Ask whether it is a "space" note or a "line" note (space).[3] Ask them which space (third). Ask them to place one finger on the first note (third space), and move it across the first phrase to find how many more C's (third-space notes) are in the phrase. Do the same with the A and F. This will help children who have trouble differentiating between "line" and "space" notes.

- What chord is made up of C, A, and F? (The F chord)
- Do you see that chord outlined any place else in the melody? (Yes, in the third phrase)
- Lynn, Susan, and Rob, get the bells for the F chord and play on phrases 1 and 3 as we sing.

---

[2]See Hints for Teaching Rote Songs, p. 186.

[3]It is important for students to become familiar with terms musicians use, in this case *in a space* and *on a line*. If students have trouble with the traditional terms, you might temporarily substitute wording that is easier for them. Show students a note that is on a line and one that is in a space, and ask them to tell in their own words where the notes are written. Then use the traditional terms, but insert the students' wording parenthetically.

- This time instead of playing your tones together, play your tone only when you see it in the melody.
- Which tone is played first? (C)
- How could you describe the first and third phrases? (They use only chord tones and are alike.)
- What tones are in the second phrase of the song? (C, B♭, G, and D)
- Do those tones outline a chord? (No)
- Would it be correct to say that in two phrases of this song, the melody outlines a chord? (Yes)
- If you had an Autoharp part for "He's Got the Whole World in His Hands," and if it were written in half notes, show me how you would strum it. Pretend you have an Autoharp in your lap as we all sing.
- Good. This time, instead of pretending to strum half notes, clasp your hands together every time you would strum an F chord and hold your hands out each time you would play a C₇ chord. Remember to sing, too.
- John, will you give out the new learning contracts? We will go over them together, so that everyone understands what the requirements are. Will you please mark your contract with a 1 for your first choice and a 2 for your second choice. You did so very well the last time we worked on contracts that we invited Mrs. Tobey's class to hear what we had learned to do. Shall we invite another class when we have completed these contracts? Let's go over them now.

LEARNING CONTRACT

Name _____ Class _____ Date _____

Song: "He's Got the Whole World in His Hands"

I will complete _____ of the following by _____:
              (how many?)   (date)

____ 1. I will practice playing the Autoharp accompaniment to "He's Got the Whole World in His Hands" until I can play it well enough to accompany group singing.

____ 2. I will practice and learn to play the following bass xylophone part as an accompaniment to group singing.

Bass Xylophone Part for "He's Got the Whole World in His Hands"

___ 3. I will practice and learn to play the following part for bells or metallophone as an accompaniment to group singing.

**Bell or Metallophone Part for
"He's Got the Whole World in His Hands"**

___ 4. I will learn to play the first and third phrases of "He's Got the Whole World in His Hands" on the recorder.

___ 5. I will learn to play the whole song on the recorder.

___ 6. I will ask three friends to play the F chord and four friends to play the C₇ chord on resonator bells. I will conduct them in playing an accompaniment as the class sings "He's Got the Whole World in His Hands."

___ 7. I will ask three friends to help me create three phrases.
   a. One phrase will use only the tones of the F chord for the melody.
   b. One phrase will use only the tones of the C₇ chord for the melody.
   c. One phrase will use both chord tones.
   We will arrange these phrases in a five-phrase piece.

___ 8. I will make up a set of motions that will show the chord changes in "He's Got the Whole World in His Hands."

HE'S GOT THE WHOLE WORLD IN HIS HANDS

BLACK SPIRITUAL

1. He's got the whole world____ in his hands,___
2. He's got the wind and rain____ in his hands,___
3. He's got both you and me____ in his hands,___

He's got the whole world ___ in his hands, ___
He's got the wind and rain ___ in his hands, ___
He's got both you and me ___ in his hands, ___

He's got the whole world ___ in his hands, ___
He's got the wind and rain ___ in his hands, ___
He's got both you and me ___ in his hands, ___

He's got the whole world in his hands. ___
He's got the whole world in his hands. ___
He's got the whole world in his hands. ___

Questions for Analysis

1. How many objectives were included in the lesson plan? Was everyone expected to master every objective? Why? Does this help or hinder individualization? How?
2. How many types of activities were included? Was everyone expected to master every activity? Why? Does this help or hinder individualization? How?
3. Was the length of time prescribed? Should it be? Why or why not?

The following plan is for a sixth-grade class that has had marked success in playing both recorders and bells.

Materials   "Joy to the World" (page 136)
Bells
Recorders
Autoharps
Maracas and drums

Concept   Most familiar melodies use the pitches of a major scale or a minor scale. Some melodies are based on a five-tone scale called the pentatonic scale. Some music uses all the twelve tones within an octave. This music is based on a tone row rather than a scale.

Objective   Experiment with various scales or arrangements of pitches to form melodies. Use rhythm patterns borrowed from "Joy to the World."

Procedure   Teach the song by rote.

JOY TO THE WORLD

WORDS AND MUSIC BY HOYT AXTON

COPYRIGHT © 1970 BY LADY JANE MUSIC. USED BY PERMISSION.

2. If I were the king of the world, tell you what I'd do,
   Throw away the fears and the tears and the jeers,
   And have a good time with you.
   Yes, I'll have a good time with you. *Refrain*

Review the meaning of the two sharps in the key signature and the scale of D major.

- Most of the songs we sing use the tones of either major or minor scales; however, there are other kinds of scales and today we are going to experiment with some of them.
- Listen as I play the refrain of "Joy to the World" using a different scale. Decide whether it uses the tones of a scale that sounds familiar to you.

Play the refrain using no sharps. Play both parts. Do not play the B♭ in the countermelody.

- Would anyone like to guess what scale tones were used?

Some students may say that the tones of a minor scale were used.

- Yes, it could be a minor scale, and it also could be a very old scale called the Dorian mode. This and other very old modes are often used in rock music.
- Take out your recorders and silently finger the refrain of "Joy to the World." That will be in the Dorian mode.
- Let's play it in the Dorian mode — without F#, C# or B♭.
- Good. That did sound different, didn't it?
- Another very old scale, the pentatonic scale, has only five tones. We can play the pentatonic scale by playing five black keys on the piano or five black bars on the bells. John, will you go to the piano and play five black keys? Put your right thumb on C# and your fingers on the next four black keys. Keep your fingers on those keys. Play each key in turn, upward and then downward. Listen for the pentatonic sound. Have you heard it before? (Yes, the students have improvised tunes using the pentatonic scale.)

- The two scales we have been experimenting with are ancient scales. Now we are going to experiment with a modern way of organizing pitches. It is not really a scale, because the tones don't sound as though they are going anywhere. They are called a tone row — and that is just what they are, a row of tones. Here is a tone row that I set up with resonator bells.

 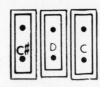  

- Mark, would you like to experiment with this tone row? Good! It is good to try new things! Play each of the tones from left to right. You may repeat a tone if you wish, but you must not go back to any you have already played. Good. That is called playing the original. Now play the tone row from right to left. You may repeat any tone, but don't go back to one you've already played. Good. That is called playing a tone row in retrograde. Now play the tone row again, but in the rhythm of the refrain of

"Joy to the World." Think the words. Don't forget that you can repeat tones. Class, will you help by clapping the rhythm very lightly? Ready, begin.

- Since very few of you really had a chance to experiment today, I have made up some learning contracts that will give everyone a chance to try out some of these other ways of organizing tones. Let's review the ways we have talked about so far today.

- You worked so well on your learning contracts last time we used them. Your work was really very good.

- Here are the contracts. John will give them out, and we will read them together so that everyone understands each option that you may take.

LEARNING CONTRACT

Name _____ *Class* _____ *Date* _____

I will complete at least one of the following options by January 25.

___ 1. I will learn to play the refrain of "Joy to the World" in the key of D major on the recorder.

___ 2. I will learn to play the countermelody to the refrain of "Joy to the World" in the key of D major on the recorder.

___ 3. I will learn to play the refrain of "Joy to the World" in the Dorian mode (no F# or C#).

___ 4. I will use the tone row on the chart and compose a piece using rhythm patterns of my choice. My composition will be for resonator bells.

___ 5. I will learn to play the Autoharp accompaniment for "Joy to the World." I will play a half-note pattern on the verse and choose my own rhythm for the refrain.

___ 6. I will practice these two rhythm instrument parts and play them with "Joy to the World."
   a. Maracas — one sound for each beat
   b. Drum — each sound lasts for two beats

___ 7. I will make up a dance to fit the AB form (verse/refrain) of "Joy to the World."

Questions for Analysis

1. In what ways does this plan take care of individual differences?
2. What background does each option require?
3. Do the options require different levels of skills in playing recorder? Bells? Rhythm instruments?
4. Do the options provide for different rates and styles of learning? How? What are some other ways to provide for individual differences?

LEARNING ACTIVITY PACKETS AND COMPUTER SOFTWARE

The most sophisticated forms of individualized instruction are those using learning activity packets and computer software. Computer software is available for music instruction and is being used to some extent in homes. Its use in public schools is limited by the number of terminals and the amount of computer time available. Learning activity packets take many forms and vary in the equipment they require. Many consist of taped lessons that have accompanying visuals on film, filmstrips, slides, or charts, or in mimeographed booklets; some are designed for use only with special equipment such as electronic keyboards and guitars. Some teachers supplement commercially prepared learning activity packets with materials they prepare themselves. Many more teachers prepare their own individualized learning activity packets.

Effective learning activity packets usually have three characteristics in common. They provide a statement of objectives; learning experiences (playing instruments, singing, listening) designed to teach or reinforce a concept or skill; and an observable means of assessing whether the concept or skill has been mastered.

EXAMPLES OF TEACHER-MADE LEARNING ACTIVITY PACKETS

Learning to play classroom instruments may pose more problems for some students than for others. To provide for those who learn more slowly, some teachers have devised their own tape-recorded packets. These packets make extra practice possible in an interesting, musical way. They can provide, for example, a recorded accompaniment for practicing only one or two tones on the recorder or for practicing the strumming of only one chord on the Autoharp. A recorder part that needs practice can be more interesting when practiced with a recording. An example is the simple recorder part for "Love" (page 25). If the slower students are given a recorder, a phonograph, and a place to work, they can have the extra practice needed to keep up with the class. If some of these children spend part of their day in a special education class, the special education teacher may be willing to provide the time, space, and equipment.

Learning packets can be based on a numbered chart that describes the music. Matching numbers are heard on the recording. Here are two examples:

PACKET 1   LEARNING ABOUT STYLE[4] (EXCERPTS)

Concept   A single musical idea may be performed in different ways, giving it a different style.

Objective Identify texture, tone color, tempo, and dynamic level in three compositions.

---

[4]Adapted from Call Chart 8: Style, in *Silver Burdett Music 5* (Morristown, N.J.: Silver Burdett Company, 1981), p. 145.

TEXTURE	TONE COLOR	TEMPO	DYNAMICS
1. Melody alone	Guitar	Fast	Getting louder
Melody with accompaniment	Strings, harp, flute	Slow	Getting softer
	Bells	Moderate	Staying the same
3. Melody alone	Guitar	Fast	Getting louder
Melody with accompaniment	Strings, harp, flute	Slow	Getting softer
	Bells	Moderate	Staying the same
4. Melody alone	Guitar	Fast	Getting louder
Melody with accompaniment	Strings, harp, flute	Slow	Getting softer
	Bells	Moderate	Staying the same

PACKET 2 **LEARNING ABOUT STYLES OF PERFORMANCE[5] (EXCERPTS)** 🔊

Concept A single musical idea may be performed in different ways, giving it a different style.

Objective Identify characteristics of melody, texture, tone color, and tempo.

MELODY	TEXTURE	TONE COLOR	TEMPO
4. Ornamented	Melody with harmony	Woman's voice with vocal accompaniment	Slow
Not ornamented	Melody alone	Adult voices	Fast
	Melody alone, then with harmony	Woman's voice with piano and organ accompaniment	Moderate
7. Ornamented	Melody with harmony	Woman's voice with vocal accompaniment	Slow
Not ornamented	Melody alone	Adult voices	Fast
	Melody alone, then with harmony	Woman's voice with piano and organ accompaniment	Moderate
8. Ornamented	Melody with harmony	Woman's voice with vocal accompaniment	Slow
Not ornamented	Melody alone	Adult voices	Fast
	Melody alone, then with harmony	Woman's voice with piano and organ accompaniment	Moderate

Questions for Analysis

1. In each of the teacher-made learning packets, was the objective clear? Was it stated in well-defined terms? How would you state each objective?
2. What was the means of assessing mastery?

---

[5]Adapted from Call Chart 6: Styles of Performance, in *Silver Burdett Music 6* (Morristown, N.J.: Silver Burdett Company, 1981), p. 95.

There are many reasons why it is important that the teacher learn how to individualize instruction for students. The most obvious reason is that individualized instruction serves the individual needs and provides for the individual capabilities of the students. This has been discussed at length in this chapter and requires no more than mention here, except to emphasize again the importance of individualizing instruction to make success possible for the special education student assigned to the regular music class. Individualized music instruction can also provide for the inclusion of music in the special education student's Individual Education Program.[6]

Another, perhaps less obvious, reason why the teacher should learn to individualize instruction is that it can help students grow as persons in at least three important ways. First, the teacher helps students develop a healthy self-concept. When students are given assignments they are able to do, they can feel good about themselves and proud of their accomplishments. Second, the teacher helps students learn the self-discipline that is necessary if they are to benefit from working independently. Finally, the teacher helps students learn to work well with others. When three or four students are responsible for completing an option on a learning contract, for example, they must learn to solve their differences of opinion quickly and fairly so they can work together to achieve a common goal. If growth in the students' human development were the only gain realized from individualized instruction, that gain alone would more than justify the time the teacher spends acquiring the skills needed to administer a program that includes individualized instruction in the classroom.

GENERALIZATIONS

The following generalizations may be drawn from the discussion of individualized instruction.

Teacher's Role The teacher assumes the role of consultant or guide as the students work independently.

Students The teacher knows as much as possible about the students' special abilities, interests, habits, home life, and so forth, in order to plan the best experiences for them.

Resource Materials The teacher knows what resource materials are available to students for both in-class and out-of-class study. The teacher is familiar with current textbook series and recordings. The teacher also investigates new materials such as computer software, programmed materials for individually prescribed instruction, and improved audio-visual aids. The teacher knows how to work a tape recorder, a filmstrip projector, and an overhead projector and is familiar with the music tapes, filmstrips, and transparencies that can be used with them.

Communication The teacher asks questions and gives instructions to students in language that they can understand.

---

[6]See Alice S. Beer and Richard Graham, *Teaching Music to the Exceptional Child: A Handbook for Mainstreaming* (Englewood Cliffs, N.J.: Prentice-Hall, Inc., 1980), pp. 27-40, and Sona D. Nocera, *Reaching the Special Learner Through Music* (Morristown, N.J.: Silver Burdett Company, 1979), pp. 3, 11.

Participation	The teacher varies learning activities, in kind and in level of difficulty, so that all students have a chance to participate in an activity and experience some degree of success.
Presentation	The teacher takes advantage of available learning materials and uses as many different teaching aids as possible.
Assignments	The teacher provides options in the kinds of assignments and in levels of difficulty, so that students can choose those best suited to their interests and abilities.
Time	The teacher provides ample time for students to grow in knowledge and skill at their own rate.
Evaluation	The teacher evaluates the growth of each student in terms of what is possible for that student rather than in terms of a common goal that may be beyond some students' capabilities.

ASSESSMENT 1 Study the following episodes and decide which generalization(s) applies to each of them.

EPISODE ONE

<u>Teacher:</u> Today you will choose your own music lesson. If you look around the room, you will see four charts posted on the walls. Each chart contains a different assignment. John, please read the assignment on chart one aloud. Tom, will you read chart two? Phyllis, please read chart three. And Harry will read chart four. Think about each assignment carefully. Decide which one you would like to do, and then get to work.

EPISODE TWO

<u>Teacher:</u> Today let's have John, Richard, and Tom sing the harmony as the rest of us sing the melody of "Joy to the World." Phillip and Pat will help them by playing their part on the resonator bells. Jane, did you remember to bring your violin? Good. Please play the melody as we sing.

EPISODE THREE

<u>Teacher:</u> Is anyone ready to play the Autoharp chords for "He's Got the Whole World in His Hands"? How much more time do you think you'll need? How can you tell when you've practiced enough?

EPISODE FOUR

<u>Teacher:</u> Ann, you will sing the fifth phrase. It begins on the third staff. The words are "When the summer hay is driest."

EPISODE FIVE

<u>Teacher:</u> How many of you have completed your learning packets? Those of you who haven't finished, continue working on them. If you have finished, go on to the next lesson. Raise your hand if you need help.

ASSESSMENT 2 Write a plan that shows how you would care for the individual differences of children. Illustrate two of the following: (a) traditional teaching methods; (b) learning contracts; (c) individualized learning packets; and (d) grouping. Plan for a fifth- or sixth-grade class that has had experience in playing recorder, guitar, bells, and Autoharp. The following song may be used or you may choose a different song.

CHUMBARA
FRENCH-CANADIAN FOLK SONG

Chum - ba - ra,_____ chum - ba - ra chum - ba - ra,_____ chum - ba - ra

chum - ba - ra,_____ chum - ba - ra chum,chum,chum,chum,chum,chum,chum,chum,

Chum - ba - ra,_____ chum - ba - ra chum - ba - ra,_____ chum - ba - ra

chum - ba - ra,_____ chum - ba - ra chum, chum!

2. Fy-do-lee   5. Say-too-mee

3. Chow-ber-ski   6. Boom-ta-da

4. Chug-ah-lee   7. Zow-lee-ski

8 *Teaching for Creativity*

CHAPTER OBJECTIVE   Write a teaching procedure that provides for the nurturing of creativity
(a) through inventing
(b) through making new combinations of musical elements, or
(c) as a means of learning.

When you plan lessons, you must provide for the creative abilities of your students. Every student has the potential for creativity, some to a greater degree than others. Recognizing that the potential for creativity exists is not enough. Except in rare instances, that potential must be stimulated or it will never be used.

WHAT IS CREATIVITY?

The word *creativity* has been used in so many different contexts that it has come to have several different meanings. A discussion of any one aspect of creativity would hardly do justice to all that can be implied when people are told that they are creative persons or that their work is creative. To give an idea of some of the ramifications of the term *creativity* — and of their implications for teaching — this discussion will treat creativity in three ways: creativity as invention, creativity as making new combinations of materials, and creativity as a means of learning or of internalizing what is learned.

CREATIVITY AS INVENTION

The dictionary says that to create means "to evolve from one's own thought or imagination; to invent." If to create is to invent, one might logically conclude that creativity means invention. The teacher who considers creativity in this light might take a clue from the saying "Necessity is the mother of invention," and structure problems and situations that require students to find inventive, imaginative solutions while using a limited number of resources. The fewer the resources students have to work with, the more imaginative they will have to be.

EPISODE ONE

<u>Teacher</u>: Pretend you are standing on a busy street corner. Think of all the different sounds you would hear. It would be easy to imitate those sounds on percussion instruments, but how many of them could you imitate if you used only your voice, your hands, and your feet? When you've thought of one, raise your hand and we'll let you try it out on us. Janice? Thank you, Janice. Does anyone have a different sound? David? Is any one else ready? Thank you for being so courteous to one another. Maybe tomorrow some more of you will share your ideas with us.

Questions for Analysis

1. What is the purpose of this kind of assignment?
2. Was the assignment given in minute detail, or did the students have considerable leeway?
3. What background or experience did the students need in order to complete the assignment?
4. Did the teacher make a value judgment?
5. Was more than one acceptable response possible? How did the students know what was acceptable?
6. Did the students have to use their imagination? How?
7. Were the students made to feel hurried? How do you know?

EPISODE TWO

<u>Teacher</u>: Are all of you back in the same groups you were in on Monday? Good. Who can state the musical problem we were working on on Monday? That's right, Peter, each group started to make up a piece that has two different sections — one section with a steady beat and meter in 2, and one section with a change in tempo. You may continue working on your pieces today. Remember that you may make your pieces for percussion instruments, for voices, or for sounds that you can make on your desks. George's group is the last to perform. Thank you. Did George's group's composition have two different sections? Was either section repeated? Did one section have a steady beat and meter in 2? Did one section have a change in tempo? Did George's group complete the assignment? Your work on this project was very good. Each group produced a very different solution to the problem. Here is an example of still another way to solve that same problem. We will listen to this music [<u>Call Chart: Rhythm</u> (record 2)][1] three times. Prepare to answer the questions that are written on the chalkboard. Cindy, will you read them, please?

1. How many sections are there?
2. Are any sections repeated?
3. List the ways in which this piece is different from the piece that your group made up. Some clues: Instruments? Length? Use of repetition? Tempo of the first section? Change of tempo in the second section?

---

[1]Adapted from Call Chart 1: Rhythm Patterns, in *Silver Burdett Music 5* (Morristown, N.J.: Silver Burdett Company, 1981), p. 15.

1. What did the students need to know in order to complete the assignment?
2. How many sound sources could they use? Was this sufficient? Why or why not?
3. Who evaluated the work?
4. Did the students have to use their imagination? How?
5. How did the teacher extend the learning?

CREATIVITY AS MAKING NEW COMBINATIONS OF MATERIALS

In her book *Creativity in Teaching,* Alice Miel treats creativity a little differently. She says:

"It [creativity] appears to be a deliberate process of making new combinations or patterning of materials."[2]

Louis M. Savary and Margaret Ehlen-Miller, in their book *Mindways: A Guide for Exploring Your Mind*[3], suggest several ideas for getting started in making new combinations. These ideas include seeking alternatives (making a different arrangement), reversing (opposite, upside down, backward), making unlikely combinations (bitonality), rearranging (changing the sequence), redefining (using a nontraditional chord structure — chords built on fourths rather than on thirds), personifying (an animal, a train, and so on).

Many of the ideas described above have been used by composers through the ages, and many of them can be used in the classroom. For example, have the students seek an alternative by substituting a new or different element for one of the elements already present in the activity. If the drum has been playing the steady beat in "Mama Don't 'Low," the students might choose to have the drum play this rhythm instead (substituting or altering the drum part):

The students might choose to add a new element to those already present in the activity. For instance, students could choose to add a percussion part to a song (add a different tone color) or add a harmony part (change the texture) or make some parts of the song fast and other parts slow (change the tempo). The teacher could have students rearrange the elements to make something new. This is somewhat like an activity that is frequently used in language arts classes, in which students are asked to "use these words to make up a sentence." In a music class, the teacher might say, "Use these tones to make up your own melody," or "Rearrange the notes in this rhythm pattern to make five new patterns."

---

[2]Alice Miel, ed., *Creativity in Teaching* (Belmont, Calif.: Wadsworth Publishing Company, 1961), p. 6.

[3]Louis M. Savary and Margaret Ehlen-Miller, *Mindways: A Guide for Exploring Your Mind* (New York: Harper & Row, Publishers, Inc., 1978), pp. 84–105.

EPISODE ONE

Teacher: Do you remember "Old Blue," the song we learned last week? Good. Let's sing the first verse. John, please play the rhythm pattern on the sticks as we sing. Very good! Look at all the different kinds of rhythm instruments on the table. As we sing the second verse of "Old Blue," try to think of another instrument that could play the rhythm pattern; or maybe even think of a different rhythm that an instrument could play or a new way to play an instrument. Does anyone have any ideas? Bill? Will you show us as we sing, Bill? Did Bill do something different? Does anyone else have an idea? Kathy? How was Kathy's idea different? Let's choose a different accompaniment for each verse.

Questions for Analysis

1. What new combinations of materials were encouraged?
2. How did the teacher encourage divergent thinking?
3. How did the teacher help the students realize that there are many ways to accompany a song?
4. What was the criterion for evaluation?

EPISODE TWO

Teacher: In our last class, you learned to play the Autoharp chords for "Michael, Row the Boat Ashore." Phyllis, would you play the chords as we sing? Very good! This time, just listen as Phyllis plays the chords for the song once more. Thank you, Phyllis. Let's have someone go to the resonator bells and play a new melody as Phyllis plays the chords for "Michael, Row the Boat Ashore." All right, Mark.

Questions for Analysis

1. What element was changed in the assignment?
2. What other changes could have been made?
3. What element or elements remained the same?

The following plan is for an upper elementary grade. It illustrates one way students could experiment with making new combinations of materials.

Materials "Banuwa" (page 148)
Rhythm instruments (including African instruments)
Melody instruments (including recorders)

Concept A musical idea can be presented in a variety of styles.

Objective Perform a song in a variety of styles by making new combinations of the elements.

Procedure Use a familiar song to show how sounds can be combined.

- You learned to sing "Banuwa" in unison very well last week. Let's sing it again to see if we need more work on it.

BANUWA

FOLK SONG FROM LIBERIA

- Good. Listen to this recording. Try to decide how the harmony is created. (By successively piling on phrases, one after another)

Have students sing the song the way it is sung on the recording.

- Is there another way we could create harmony? (By playing an Autoharp accompaniment)

Have someone play the Autoharp accompaniment.

- Do you remember hearing "Amazing Grace" performed in three different styles? (See Learning About Styles of Performance, page 140, record 2). First it was sung by a woman, with an ornamented melody and with a vocal accompaniment. Then it was sung by a group of adults. Finally it was sung by a woman, with an ornamented melody and with piano and organ accompaniment. Listen to the recording again, to help you remember it.
- Let's think of different ways we could perform "Banuwa." We will list them on the chalkboard.

Students may need some help. Clues can be given by asking such questions as, "Can we change the accompaniment? How?" or "Can we change the melody? How?"

Students may suggest ideas like the following for performing "Banuwa": Change the instruments in the accompaniment, change the tempo, change the dynamics, alternate solo and chorus by phrase, change the rhythm of the melody, decorate or ornament the melody, use different harmony.

Experiment with each suggestion. This can be done either with the whole group or in small groups (See Chapter 6, "Teaching Large and Small Groups"). It could also be done with learning contracts (See Chapter 7, "Individualizing Instruction").

1. What did the students have to know in order to take part in the lesson?
2. What elements are included in the suggestions for changes? Can you think of others? What are they?
3. How did the teacher help the students? Are there other ways? What are they?
4. What did students learn from this experience?

CREATIVITY AS A MEANS OF LEARNING

Children grasp and internalize a concept more readily when they can show the workings of that concept in an original composition. There are many ways to facilitate and nurture creativity in classroom activities. Composition is only one of several, but it is a highly important one since it can involve many other musical tasks.

At first, it is necessary to set rather narrow limits for the student composer. The number of possibilities for rhythm, melody, harmony, tone color, and form in a composition is so vast that the student could easily be overwhelmed and give up. Working in small groups, with a teacher as facilitator and with realistic limits, the young composer can begin to develop original ideas and try them.

Using the act of composing as a musical means rather than as an end behavior requires a rather structured preparation on the part of the teacher. Here are some ideas:

1. Limit the size of the group. Five to seven students can be a workable size.
2. Take care in the assignment of students to a group. Avoid putting too many leaders or too many followers into one group.
3. Before assigning group activities in composition, become acquainted with the degree of self-control each student has.
4. Assign specific but separate tasks to each group. Some things could be the same, but some things must be different.
5. View group tasks in composition as possible evaluative tools at the end of a unit of work. "Compose a percussion piece in duple or triple meter using quarter, half, and eighth notes and equivalent rests" could be an assignment after the study of meter and duration relationships.
6. At times, assign only one group to work on a project. The rest of the class can be working on some other activity. In this case, be careful to assign students who can work together without too much consultation with you, since you will be busy with the other students in the class.

Preparation

One of the easier ways to initiate group composition is to decide on the limits of the composition and prepare directions on index cards. Here are two examples for the same class activity with two different groups.

GROUP 1

Limits: One pitch — for example, only C's
Length of composition: Not less than 30 seconds or more than 45 seconds
Form: AB
Tone color: Alto xylophone for pitch; any nonpitched percussion for other events
Rhythm patterns: Quarter and eighth notes in any pattern. Also use rests; they're interesting!
Meter: Duple or triple for section A; clock time (no meter) for section B
Scoring: Make a musical score using traditional symbols

GROUP 2

Limits: One pitch — for example, only C's
Length of composition: Not less than 30 seconds or more than 45 seconds
Form: Free
Tone color: Piano for pitch; nonpitched mouth sounds for other events
Rhythm patterns: Long and short sounds in any combination
Meter: None; use clock time throughout
Reminder: Use silence as well as sound
Scoring: Make a score using any symbols or drawings you wish

In both cases, the composition shows the inventive use of only one pitch, is not longer than 45 seconds or shorter than 30 seconds, and requires the group to make some kind of score of the composition. Each group is assigned a different form, and there is variety in the use of tone color, rhythm pattern, and meter.

Before you give your students assignments such as these, be sure they have been introduced to the things they will need to know in order to complete the assignment: the meaning of AB form, free form, and meter, as well as the relationship among the notes and rests they will use in rhythm patterns.

Getting Started

- Today we're going to use some of the things we've learned so far. I have some cards for you to use in composing a piece of music. Joey, Denise, Al, you will be group 1.

Divide the class into groups and number the groups (usually four groups will be sufficient). Give one index card with directions for composition to each group, and assign the groups to separate work areas.

- Don't show your card to anyone outside your group. Keep your ideas secret until you perform your piece. Denise, please be responsible for the card in your group.
- Remember to follow all the directions on your cards. You will have to decide who will play what instruments and how you will score your piece. All of you have such good ideas that I'm sure you'll have no problem making up a piece. I'll give you the rest of this period to get started.

Move around among the groups and be certain they understand exactly what they are to do.

At first, it may be necessary to encourage a type of musical scoring that does not use notation. For example, the score for group 2 (page 150) could look like this:

	5″	10″	10″	5″	5″	1″
PIANO	PLAY ANY C AS FAST AS YOU CAN ▬▬ ▪ ▪	Quiet	START PATTERN SLOW AND SOFT. GET FAST AND LOUD. USE A LOT OF C'S. ▪ ▪ ▬ ▬	SOFT TO LOUD HIGH LOW	REALLY FAST ▬ ▬ ▬ ▬	ONE LOUD THUMP
TONGUE CLUCK	LOUD ▬ ▬ SLOW	FAST BUT SOFT ▪ ▬ ▬ ▬	Quiet	Quiet	▬▬ ▪ ▪ ▪ ▪ ▬ GET LOUD	LOUD CLUCK
HISS	DO THIS A LOT LOUD ▪ ▪ ▬ ▬	SLOW AND SOFT ▬ ▬ ▬	Quiet	SOFT TO LOUD ▬▬▬▬▬▬	SHORT AND SHARP ▪ ▪ FAST	LOUD HISS
GROAN	⋀⋀⋀⋀ LOUD	Quiet	∿∿∿∿ START SOFT	∿∿∿ AND GET LOUD	∿∿	BIG GROAN

Discuss with students the purposes of a score: to help the group remember the order of events; to specify the tone colors they have chosen; to enable another group to play the piece without help from those who wrote it; and to provide for changes to be made during the composing process.

ANOTHER DAY

- Let's get to work in our groups. In fifteen minutes let's have a progress report from each group. Then we will work on some other things we started last week.

It is usually not a good idea to spend the entire class time for several days in succession on group composition.

ANOTHER DAY

- From your progress reports last time, I notice that you're almost ready to perform your pieces. Take about fifteen minutes now to rehearse and check your scores. Here's some masking tape. Put your scores on the chalkboard.

At the end of fifteen minutes, use a prearranged signal such as flicking the light switch or playing a chord on the piano to attract attention.

- Group 2, that really was a fine performance. Class, could you follow their score as they played? Could you hear each part clearly? Did group 3 play exactly what was written in their score?

Give opportunities for the pieces to be played several times. Ask questions that will lead to rethinking the compositions and trying new ideas without making value judgments.

Suggestions for Compositions

1. Use any five pitches from the resonator bell set and make up a one-minute piece.
2. Use a verse of four lines, or a haiku, or a cinquain, and with the Autoharp only, provide an accompaniment to the reading of the poem. Remember that there are many ways to play the Autoharp.
3. Use the three pitches the class can play on the recorder (G, A, and B) and make a score for a composition in triple meter, eight measures in length. Use traditional notation to score your piece.
4. Using paper only, make up a piece by rattling, crumpling, tearing, and snapping the paper. Use drawings and symbols to make a score.
5. Using claves, large drum, and maracas only, make up a percussion piece in duple meter.
6. Play the following chord progression on the Autoharp or guitar. Repeat it many times while someone improvises a melody on bells. Invent your own way of scoring it.

C   A min. D min.   G₇   end on C

7. Use someone's birth date as the basis for a melody. Then make up a composition using that melody. Let each number in the birth date match one of the tones of a major scale. For example, if the birth date is 8–26–71 and your composition is based on the D major scale, you could work out a melody this way.

1 2 3 4 5 6 7 8

Questions for Analysis

1. Study the suggestions for compositions. How does each one help students internalize a concept? Is more than one concept involved?
2. If students have difficulty with any part of a composition, what should the teacher do? How should this affect the teacher's future planning?

THE IMPORTANCE OF CREATIVE EXPERIENCES

Besides the fact that classroom experiences requiring creative responses help the students to become inventive, provide practice in making new combinations of materials, and serve as a vehicle for learning, there are other reasons for including them in the music program.

First, creative experiences give students an opportunity to make musical judgments. Every time students make up their own pieces, they must make decisions. They must decide what sounds they will use and in what order they will use them; they must decide whether the sounds will be used separately or in combination with other sounds; they must decide whether the sounds will be loud or soft, fast or slow, connected or detached; they must decide whether silences will occur; and so forth. When they have finished their compositions, they must decide whether the work is good enough, whether it needs to be changed, or perhaps even whether it needs to be started over again. As creators, students must decide whether the piece represents their very best efforts or whether it just barely fulfills the assignment.

Second, creative experiences give students great leeway in fulfilling assignments. They permit them to draw on all they know about music to make their compositions interesting and satisfying. An instruction given in September to make up a percussion piece in ABA form may result in a piece in which a drum plays first one rhythm, then another, and then the first rhythm again. But as students grow and develop in their knowledge of music, that same instruction to write a piece in ABA form may result in a piece that reflects students' understanding of tempo (section A is fast, section B slow); dynamics (section A is soft, section B is loud); tone color (section A is scored for triangle, section B for drum); and so forth.

Third, creative experiences provide students with a greater chance for success. If the teacher asks students to identify the form of "Clap Your Hands," students can only be right if the answer is "AB." But if the teacher asks the students to make up a piece in AB form, their chances of being right are multiplied many times over. Anything that is written, no matter how simple or complex, will be the "right" answer as long as the composition has two different sections.

Finally, creative experiences help the teacher assess what the students know and are able to do, since they only function creatively at their personal level of understanding and skill. Some students will need review and reinforcement. Others apparently will make intuitive leaps and demonstrate insight far beyond the classroom learning experiences and the teacher's expectations.[4] Whether due to intuitive leaps or other causes, the expressions of children can be surprisingly sophisticated. Creative involvement should definitely be a part of the school music experience.

GENERALIZATIONS

The following generalizations may be drawn from the discussion of creativity.

Respect Every creative effort must be treated with respect and be given serious consideration by both teacher and students. No creative endeavor must ever be subject to ridicule.

---

[4]See "Creativity and the Right Brain," pp. 37–51, in Thomas R. Blakeslee, *Right Brain: A New Understanding of the Unconscious Mind and Its Creative Powers* (New York: Doubleday & Company, Inc., 1980) and "Gateways to Creativity," pp. 84–85, in Louis M. Savary and Margaret Ehlen-Miller, *Mindways: A Guide for Exploring Your Mind* (New York: Harper & Row, Publishers, Inc., 1978).

Problem Solving	The teacher must be certain that the problem is stated clearly and that the students understand what they are supposed to do. It should be possible to solve the problem in several ways. Refinement comes through experimentation.
Time	The teacher must allow sufficient time for students to carry out the assignment without pressure or hurrying. The students should be encouraged to give progress reports when they have not completed the assignment.
Materials	Except when the teacher wants students to find their own materials, many resources should be provided. The teacher should suggest additional resources as they are needed.
Thinking	The teacher should encourage students to think creatively — to inquire, explore, search, experiment, analyze, plan, summarize, generalize, and evaluate. Diversity of thought rather than conformity should be encouraged.
Speculation	The teacher should encourage students to hypothesize and to forecast probable results.
Questions	Questions should be open-ended. The teacher should not expect one specific answer but should be willing to accept any answer that is logical.
Evaluation	Teacher and students should evaluate early creative efforts in terms of whether or not those efforts fulfill the assignment, not in terms of their own worth. Value judgments should be delayed until students have had many opportunities to work creatively. In creative work, the process is often more important than the product.

ASSESSMENT 1 Study the following episodes and decide which generalization(s) applies to each of them.

EPISODE ONE

Teacher: Who remembers what an ostinato is? Can anyone give us an example of an ostinato? Who can give us another example? Today as you work in your groups, you are to do two things. First, decide on an ostinato; second, make up a melody to go with it.

EPISODE TWO

Teacher: Yesterday we used bell chords to accompany "I'm Gonna Sing" and discovered that the tones of the chords were a third apart. Can anyone think of a different way to build chords? Kathy? Tony? Do you have a different idea, Mary? As you work in your groups today, try to build chords with tones that are not a third apart. When you're ready, we'll see how your new chords sound with "I'm Gonna Sing."

EPISODE THREE

Teacher: You won't have time to finish your composition today, but perhaps each group leader could give us a progress report. Let's begin with Bob's group. Thank you. Between now and Thursday, see how much you can find out about ostinato. You might try listening to the radio or to recordings to find out how today's composers use ostinato. How else can you find out more about it? Yes, you could look in your music book or you could ask a musician. I'll look forward to hearing about your discoveries.

EPISODE FOUR

Teacher: Make up a melody that moves upward by step and down? leap.

EPISODE FIVE

Teacher: That was very good! How fast do you think this song should go? Harley? Can you conduct us so that we can try singing it at your speed? Does anyone think it should be sung at a different tempo? All right, Martha. We'll try singing as you conduct. Would anyone like to try conducting at still another tempo? Which tempo seemed best for the song? Why do you think so, Nancy? Does anyone have a different idea?

ASSESSMENT 2   Write a teaching procedure that provides for creative expression in one of the three ways described in this chapter. Identify (1) the age level of the students, (2) the background needed to be successful, and (3) the musical learning to be gained. Use "Long John" or a song of your choice.

LONG JOHN   BLUES SONG

SOLO ... CHORUS

With his shin - y blade,____ With his shin - y blade,____

Got it in his hand,____ Got it in his hand,____

Gon - na chop out the live oaks, Gon - na chop out the live oaks,

That are in this land,____ That are in this land.____

He's Long John,____ He's Long John,____ He's long gone,____

He's long gone,___ He's gone, gone,___ He's gone, gone,___

Like a tur-key in the corn,___ Like a tur-key in the corn,___

With his long clothes on,___ With his long clothes on,___

He's long gone,___ He's long gone,___ He's long gone,___

He's long gone,___ He's gone, He's long gone.___

9 Discipline in Music Classes

List steps that a teacher can take to
(a) prevent discipline problems,
(b) control inappropriate behavior, and
(c) modify inappropriate behavior.

PREVENTING DISCIPLINE PROBLEMS

A teacher may know all there is to know about the subject, prepare the most thorough lesson plans, and yet not be a successful teacher. Success in the classroom depends on much more than intellectual ability or good musicianship, even though both are important. It depends on knowing how to deal with students as persons. The ability to gain respect and the ability to set and maintain limits of acceptable behavior are central to the prevention of discipline problems.

ESTABLISHING MUTUAL RESPECT

When mutual respect is established among the people who are to work together, many discipline problems are prevented. In the classroom, mutual respect and interpersonal regard must be a three-way interaction, for the classroom can provide an atmosphere that is conducive to learning only if the teacher respects the students, the students respect their teacher, and the students respect their fellow students.

Teachers who do not show respect for students, who remain aloof, or who feel superior to students cannot expect to have a successful classroom experience. It is imperative that teachers have a genuine concern for students, and it is equally imperative that this concern be communicated to the students. As teachers go about their daily business, there are countless opportunities to show that they care about their students and that they respect them. Teachers show respect and caring by their general attitude. They have an air of confidence, a pleasant, relaxed manner, a way of communicating the idea that learning is important and that teachers and pupils learn together. Such an attitude is far more conducive to learning than an attitude that says, "I'm here to do the teaching; whether or not you learn is entirely up to you."

Teachers show that they care by the extra things they do, such as coming in a few minutes early or taking time on their lunch hour to help students solve problems. They show they care when they tell a student who hasn't done the assignment to stop by after class and talk about it, rather than reprimanding the student in front of the class. Teachers show that they care when they react to a disruptive student's "fresh" answer with "Are you sure that's what you meant to say, Tom? Think about it . . ." instead of "I should have expected an answer like that from you." In these and in many other ways teachers tell students, "I respect you; I'm concerned about you; I care about you."

Students' respect is a very precious thing, and it is something that every teacher must earn. Students have wonderful instincts when it comes to "figuring out" their teachers. They can sense whether a teacher feels unsure; they can tell when a teacher is insincere; they can detect little gestures of annoyance that tell them a teacher doesn't think they are very intelligent; they can pick up the sarcasm, ridicule, or even contempt in a teacher's tone of voice. Students respect a teacher who is confident, who is thoroughly prepared, who lets them know exactly what is expected, who treats them fairly, and who shows respect for them.

Students must learn to respect one another if the classroom experience is to be a happy one. Teachers can encourage mutual respect among students by setting a good example in the way they relate to students. For example, a teacher can encourage mutual respect by praising the things that students do well and by refraining from criticizing the things they do poorly; by preparing the class for a new class member; by determining each student's special talent and encouraging it; and by making learning a team effort in which each student's progress becomes everyone's concern, instead of letting it become a competitive effort in which each student tries to outdo the others.

Mutual respect is important because it promotes a warm, accepting climate that is vital to learning. When the teacher is relaxed and helpful, when students don't have to worry about being criticized and berated in front of their fellow students, when everyone's efforts are considered worthy, students are in a good environment for learning.

Mutual respect is important because it gives each student a feeling of personal worth. If students know that what they learn *matters* to the teacher and to their fellow students, their desire to please will increase and along with it, motivation to learn.

Finally mutual respect is important because it helps students develop self-discipline. When students have respect for one another, when they care about one another, when they feel responsible for helping one another to learn, the amount of disruptive behavior in the classroom decreases. In an atmosphere where everyone's rights and opinions are respected, discipline is not a serious problem.

SETTING LIMITS OF BEHAVIOR

Letting students know exactly what behavior will be tolerated and what behavior will not is another important key to preventing discipline problems. Some teachers set forth the rules for acceptable behavior. Others ask students to help make the rules. There is no one way to set limits for behavior. It depends on the teacher and on the age and character of the class. Some teachers do not make rules but rather handle each desirable and undesirable act as it occurs. When this is done consistently, children soon learn what is acceptable and what is not. If there are too many rules, the teacher may spend too much time enforcing them rather than teaching and sharing the enjoyment of music. There are some guidelines that should be considered:

1. Convey the idea from the beginning that students' behavior is important; that you take their actions seriously and expect them to act in an acceptable manner.

2. Be consistent. Students must have the security of knowing what is expected of them in the classroom. The teacher who seeks students' opinions one day and ignores them the next, or lets students chew gum on Monday but reprimands them when they chew it on Tuesday, cannot help but confuse students and encourage undesirable behavior.

3. Be calm. If your voice becomes loud and strident, students will become nervous and irritated. If you display lack of ease by pacing or constantly moving about the room or by talking incessantly, students will reflect your agitation in their behavior.

4. Be alert. You cannot become so wrapped up in the content of the lesson that you fail to consider the physical comfort of the students. You must be able to tell that the room is too warm, or that children have been sitting or standing too long, or that they need a change of activity. During the course of the lesson, station yourself at various places in the room so that you can be aware of what is going on in all parts of the room.

5. Be confident. You must be secure enough to know that you don't have to nag students to get them to do their work or abide by the rules.

6. Be positive. You should make "Praise, not blame" your motto. If the teacher says, "John's group isn't ready, as usual," it takes John's group even longer to get ready. But if the teacher says, "Good for your group, John, you're all ready," John's group will hurry to get ready the next time, too.

7. Be inventive. Plan occasional games and surprises that break up the monotony of routine. Change bulletin boards frequently. (Bulletin boards can be good teaching aids.) Change seating plans from time to time, and keep lessons interesting by using a variety of teaching aids — films, filmstrips, television, supplementary books, spirit masters, and so forth.

8. Keep the lesson moving, and keep all students involved. If there are times when nothing is happening or the lesson is moving too slowly, students will react in undesirable ways.

9. Provide time for students to explore the various sounds that can be made on percussion instruments and other instruments in the room. If students have an opportunity to satisfy their curiosity about the sounds of instruments, they may not be so tempted to beat the drum or bang the piano every time they pass by. (A prearranged signal should bring this type of exploratory activity to a close.)

10. Get the lesson off to a good start. If you greet each child at the door, the students will not rush into the room, making it necessary to waste precious minutes quieting them down before the lesson can begin. The way a lesson begins may set the climate for the entire period.

Establishing mutual respect and communicating exactly the behavior that is expected are far more complex than can be explained in words. Body language, facial expressions, and mannerisms all affect the way children perceive their teacher. Nonetheless, words do make a difference.

The following teaching procedure illustrates at least two ways that a teacher may choose to talk to children. Be ready to answer the Questions for Analysis.

Materials	"Get on Board" (page 12, record 1) Space for movement Rhythm instruments
Concept	Music can be organized into sections, that may be alike or different.
Objectives	Identify like and unlike sections by making the same motions for like sections and different motions for different sections. Select instruments of two different tone colors to illustrate like and unlike sections.

Procedure

Teacher 1	Teacher 2
• Every person in Row 1 has a cleared desk. Good for you.	• Row 2, why haven't you cleared your desks? We always have to wait for you.
• I know there are good listeners in this room. Who can tell what kind of travel this song tells about? Katrina? Yes, very good.	• What kind of travel does this song tell about? Listen carefully, don't make it necessary to play the record three times before you get it.
• Listen again. Can you hear a place in the song where the conductor is saying something to the children?	• Listen again. What is the conductor saying to the children?
• Good.	• Yes. That is right.
• Make a motion that you think a conductor might make as he tells the children to "get on board." Stand. Look around you to be sure you have enough space to move. Ian, will you please move this way a little? Good. Thank you for using only your own space. No accidents!	• Make a motion that you think a conductor might make as he tells the children to "get on board." Stand. Don't bump into anyone.
• John, I noticed you stopped your motion in the middle of the song. Why? (That part did not tell about the children.) Good. You really listened well.	• Why did you all bump into one another? Sit down. We will not do that activity again until you learn not to bump into each other. Sit down.
• Let's listen again — this time for the part that doesn't tell about the children. When you hear it, make a different motion. Watch your space!	• Listen again, this time for the part that doesn't tell about the children. When you hear it, raise your hand.

- Did you make the same motion twice? (Yes) Where? (At the beginning and at the end) Let's make our motions one more time as we listen. Be sure to make a different motion where the music sounds different. If you are not sure, watch John's group. Good, everyone got it that time. There are two parts of that music that are alike. Sit down. Show when you are ready for your next direction.
- We have four kinds of instruments on the table: triangles, drums, wood blocks, and maracas. You have played each of them many times. As you listen, pretend to play one of those instruments.

Observe the children. When you see someone playing in rhythm, hand that child an instrument.

- We heard maracas and drums. Can you think of a way that we could show with the instruments the parts that are alike and the parts that are different? (Play the same instruments on parts that are alike) Good. Drums will play on the parts that are alike, and maracas will play on parts that are different. Who will play first? (Drums) Everyone else, pretend to play one of the two instruments.
- Every person that had an instrument handled it very well! Next time those who did not have a chance to play, will. Children in the first row, quietly put your maracas back on the table. Children in the second row. Children in the third row. I hope you all noticed how well the children handled the instruments. They played them only when asked. They put them carefully on the table. They did not run. They were super! Let's give them a hand! I know the rest of the class can do just as well when they play the instruments next time.

- There are two parts in the music that are alike. The middle part is different.

- Let's see if you can play your instruments better than you can do motions.

- There are two parts to this song that are alike. We have maracas and drums on the table. Everyone in rows 1, 2, and 3 go to the table and get a drum. Don't run! Go back! This class doesn't do anything right. You can't play rhythm instruments until you learn how to handle them.

1. Which comments do you think build mutual respect?
2. Which comments demonstrate that the teacher is communicating the behavior that is expected?
3. What further suggestions do you have for this procedure?

CONTROLLING INAPPROPRIATE BEHAVIOR

Teachers may take every precaution they know and still find that problems arise. It is important that the teacher act in some positive way at the first sign of trouble, for disruptive behavior that is ignored does not always disappear; it can get worse. Many teachers have found the following suggestions helpful.

1. Call for structured responses that eliminate choices. For example, when using instruments, have a specific place where instruments are to be when not in use (such as at the top of the desk, or under the chair). Be consistent in the signal for picking up the instruments ("Ready, pickup"). Insist that students only play on signal ("Ready, play"). With some classes it may be necessary to isolate and practice the mechanics of handling the instruments until everyone understands the necessity for following the procedure. When teaching movement activities, be very clear about the signal for starting and the signal for stopping. Identify the exact space to be used. Some classes cannot handle choices and need very structured modes of response.

2. Plan transitions carefully. When moving from one activity to another, carefully plan your movements and the movements of the class. To maintain control, have every piece of equipment at your fingertips, ready for use. Use prepared charts rather than turning your back on the class to write on a chalkboard. Keep the whole class within your line of vision during the transition from one activity to another. (The fact that you have everyone within your vision can easily be communicated by the body language of stretching or leaning in the direction in which you are looking.)

   Make it clear exactly what the class is to do to get ready for the next activity. Give directions concisely and firmly. Leave no "dead" time between activities. The mechanics of smooth transitions must be carefully planned, especially when dealing with a troublesome class. Such classes need the security of knowing exactly what you consider appropriate behavior.

3. Plan different types of experiences for a change of pace. Within each class period plan for some work that requires concentration, some quiet activities, and some physical or manual activities. Work that requires concentration could include learning a new fingering for recorder or learning a new song. Quiet activities could include listening, or the introduction of music that has a quieting effect — either sung, played, or listened to. Rhythmic activities or playing instruments can fill the need for physical or manual activity. Keep in mind the developmental levels of the children in order to plan suitable change-of-pace activities.[1]

4. Change the mood of the room by praising the children for something they have done well (or even fairly well). If the children have learned a new

---

[1]See Theories of Child Growth and Development, p. 195.

song, you might ask the principal or assistant principal, another teacher, or another group of children to come and hear them sing it. It may happen that no one can come at the moment, but even so you have expressed confidence in the students. (You should be certain to have someone hear the song in the next music class.)

You might also change the mood in the room by switching to an activity that you know the class enjoys. You might try involving the class in singing one song after another without stopping between songs. A list of page numbers on the chalkboard is all that is necessary. Try letting the music work its own magic.

5. Help the negative child find positive outlets. Some children periodically need to be away from the group for a short time. One teacher who has such a boy has worked out an arrangement with the principal. Whenever she senses that the child is becoming tense, she sends him to the office, on an errand. The child walks to the office, delivers a note or book to the principal, receives the principal's thanks, and is ready to join the group again when he gets back to the room. Another teacher deals with a hyperactive girl by giving her special assignments. For instance, she may compose a piece at the piano while the rest of the class is working in groups. Later, she is invited to share her composition with the class.

6. Remain calm. Sometimes a quiet, calm, firm manner will restore order. A few minutes of quiet may be all that is needed to relieve tension.

Study the following teaching procedure. Be ready to answer the Questions for Analysis.

Material   "Hold On"
Recorders
Rhythm instruments

Concept   Melodies may have short patterns that are repeated.

Objective   Learn how to play low D on the recorder. Identify, and then play on recorder, the repeated melodic phrases in "Hold On."

Procedure   • Today we are going to continue to work on the song "Hold On." Follow my motions as we sing verse 1. Watch closely, I may surprise you.

HOLD ON   AMERICAN FOLK SONG

Keep your hand on____ that plow,____
Keep your hand on____ that plow,____

Hold on, hold on, hold on.
Hold on, hold on, hold on.
Hold on, hold on,

Bet - ter keep your hand right on____ that plow,____

Hold on, hold on, hold on.

3. Keep on plowin' and don't you tire,
   Ev'ry row goes higher and higher.
   Keep your hand on that plow,
   Hold on, hold on, hold on. *Refrain*

4. If that plow stays in your hand,
   Head you straight for the promised land.
   Keep your hand on that plow,
   Hold on, hold on, hold on. *Refrain*

- Clap the rhythm of the melody except on the words "Hold on, hold on, hold on." Slap your thighs both times this pattern occurs.

- Good! Everyone got it. Take your recorder out of its case. Place it at the top of your desk in rest position. Good. You follow directions better every day. What position do you take when you pick up your recorder? Craig? (Hold it against your chin — not in the mouth.) Correct. Everyone ready, chin position.

- We are going to learn to play D. Look at my hands. Are all the holes covered? Amy? (All except one) Good. Everyone look at Amy's hands. Squeeze the holes. Examine your fingers. Can you see where each was pressed against a hole? You should have a small circle.

- We are going to play the echo game. Recorders in playing position. Ready, position. Listen first.

Play D, using several different patterns, including the pattern for "Hold On" (five quarter notes followed by a half note).

- Good. Recorders in chin position. Ready, chin position.
- Look at my fingers as I play.

Play the pattern for "Hold on, hold on, hold on."

- Which phrase of the song did I play? ("Hold on, hold on, hold on")

- Practice fingering that phrase. Ready, begin.
- Good. Listen first and then play it after me.

Play the phrase several times and have the class echo it. When they are playing it well, have them play it with the recording.

- Put your recorders in their cases. You have worked well and hard today. Now we are going to sing one of your favorite songs.

Questions for Analysis

1. Can you find evidence of the teacher's having planned for any of the following?
   a. Structured responses
   b. Smooth transitions
   c. Change of pace
   d. Change of mood
   e. A negative or hyperactive child

2. In each case above, what did the teacher say that made such planning evident?

MODIFYING INAPPROPRIATE BEHAVIOR

If trouble should persist with a few students or the entire class, find out as much as possible about the students. Try to find the musical level of the students and let the music speak directly to them. It may be that the music is either too difficult or too simple to be challenging or interesting. Many beginning teachers talk too much about music or try to deal with it in an abstract manner. Children rebel at this approach because they do not have the facility to work with words or abstractions — they need activity. With some difficult classes, it may be necessary to plan lessons that are completely activity-centered. Without talking about music at all, let children sing or play. Use the most appealing music you can find. Use a variety of music, including popular music. Nothing will be gained until you have won the children over.

Try to get to know the children as persons. Have conferences with disruptive children. Appeal to them and, remembering that most children really want to do well in school, try to discover the reasons for lack of cooperation in class.

Confer with other teachers, the principal, the guidance counselor, and the special education teacher if you are not reaching the mainstreamed children. Try to initiate some concerted action to deal with the problem behavior. Talk to the parents of disruptive children and elicit their help in finding solutions. Invite parents to visit the class and even participate in the music lessons.

Adapt some of the techniques music therapists use in their approach to behavior modification. The following are some suggestions that may be helpful in dealing with disruptive individuals or an extremely difficult class.

1. Pinpoint the behavior you want to modify. If you are concerned with one or two students, the pinpointed behavior might be having the students stay in their seats, rather than roaming around the room. If you are

concerned with a whole class, the pinpointed behavior might be handling rhythm instruments roughly, or playing them at the wrong times. If a class seems to work well for a while and then falls apart, analyze exactly what happens at that point in the lesson and pinpoint the event or events that cause the breakdown.

2. Count the number of times the inappropriate behavior occurs in a music lesson so that you have a baseline from which to measure progress. For example, if on October 1 the inappropriate behavior occurs ten times in the lesson, and by November 1 the count has been lessened by three, you will know that you are making progress. Without a count, small steps in progress may go unnoticed.

3. Decide on a procedure that rewards and reinforces appropriate behavior and ignores inappropriate behavior (when possible). The rewards might include choosing a song or an instrument or taking an instrument out of the music room to practice; verbal reinforcement and positive comments by the teacher, smiles, pats on the back, handshakes, and applause; or points earned toward a special concert or field trip. If points are to be counted toward tangible rewards, students must know exactly how points are to be earned, and they must be convinced that points are awarded fairly. Some teachers use behavior charts stating the behavior that is to be modified. Daily progress toward modifying the behavior is recorded on the chart. Behavior charts may be devised for the whole class or for individuals. If a behavior chart is used for a whole class, be sure to avoid letting the class become antagonistic toward one or two disruptive children. Deal with those children individually. The following sample behavior chart is for a whole class.

GRADE 4 — ROOM 100

(The pinpointed behavior)	Dates			
	1/14	1/17	1/21	1/24
Took seats promptly	✔	✔		✔
Played instruments only on signal		✔		✔

Charts for individuals should be held in the strictest confidence between the individual and the teacher. The marking should be done with the individual as soon as possible after the lesson. The following sample behavior chart is for an individual.

JOHN JOHNSON

(The pinpointed behavior)	Dates			
	2/21	2/24	2/28	3/3
Participated		✔	✔	✔
Did not move chair	✔		✔	

GENERALIZATIONS

The following generalizations may be drawn from the discussion of discipline in music classes.

Teacher The teacher works together with the students as a member of the team.

Attitude Teacher and students are relaxed, cheerful, and pleasant.

Patience Teacher and students take the time to listen to one another.

Respect Mutual respect between teacher and students and between students and fellow students is evident in the courtesy and consideration shown.

Agreement Teacher and students consider all opinions in trying to come to an agreement.

Mistakes Teacher and students are tolerant of one another's mistakes and use them to promote learning.

Students' Problems Teacher and students accept personal problems and handicaps with consideration.

Success The teacher provides materials that are within the capabilities of students, praising individual effort, improvement, and achievement.

Evaluation The teacher gives positive, constructive criticism and encourages students to evaluate their own work.

Setting Limits Students know what is acceptable and unacceptable behavior.

Consistency The teacher is consistent in enforcing the limits of behavior.

Fairness The teacher is fair in enforcing the limits of behavior.

Control The teacher takes the necessary steps to control the inappropriate behavior of a few students to protect the learning environment for the class.

Modification The teacher uses every resource available to modify undesirable behavior.

ASSESSMENT 1 The following teaching procedure illustrates some ways to prevent, control, or modify inappropriate behavior in the music classroom. Study the procedure and see how many ways you can identify. Support your reasoning.

Materials "Che Che Koolay" (page 168, record 2)
Rhythm instruments

Concept The phrases in a song may be the same length or different lengths.

Objectives 1. (Primary) Identify phrases in a song and determine whether they are the same or different in length.
2. (Secondary) Use only assigned space for rhythmic activities.

Procedure Have the students stand and stretch their arms out in front of them, then move their arms to each side to test their space. If some students are touching, assign them to places that are large enough to swing their arms without invading anyone else's space. Ask students to pretend that they have a long pencil in each hand and extending their arms, draw an imaginary circle on the floor around them. This imaginary (magic) circle defines their own space for the activities that follow.

Teach the chant by using the recording and have students mimic your motions.

CHE CHE KOOLAY

SINGING GAME FROM GHANA

FROM HI. NEIGHBOR (BOOK 2) BY UNITED STATES FOR UNICEF. UNITED NATIONS. N.Y. USED BY PERMISSION.

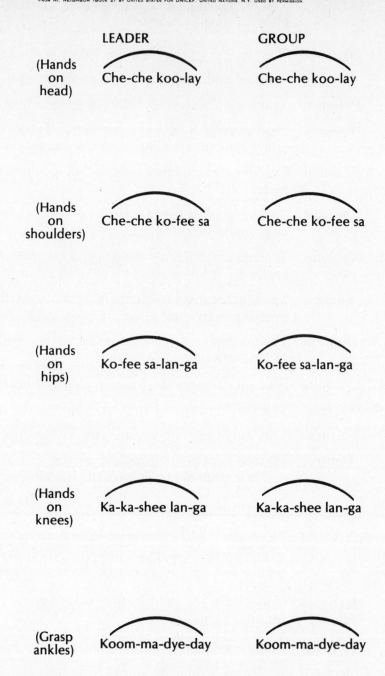

	LEADER	GROUP
(Hands on head)	Che-che koo-lay	Che-che koo-lay
(Hands on shoulders)	Che-che ko-fee sa	Che-che ko-fee sa
(Hands on hips)	Ko-fee sa-lan-ga	Ko-fee sa-lan-ga
(Hands on knees)	Ka-ka-shee lan-ga	Ka-ka-shee lan-ga
(Grasp ankles)	Koom-ma-dye-day	Koom-ma-dye-day

When students have learned to follow the leader in making the motions and have learned to sing the chant, choose a student leader to make up different motions. Remind the student leader to use only the allotted space.

As the student leads the class, draw phrase marks on the chalkboard like those shown in the chant.

• How many phrases are there in this chant? (Ten)
• Are the phrases the same or different lengths? (Same)

- Good. This class gets a check mark for remembering to use only your space for the game we just played. That makes three checks this week! You may take your seats.
- Emil, here is a drum. Play the rhythm of the words of the first phrase of "Che Che Koolay." Good. Play that again. The class will echo the rhythm by clapping.
- I am looking for someone who is following directions to play a different instrument on the second phrase.

Continue until all the phrases have been played, using a variety of body sounds for the class responses. Collect the instruments.

- Last week some of you played the rhythm of your names on instruments. Emil, let's hear how your name will sound on your drum. (E-mil Stra-vin-ski) Good. Make a phrase by playing that rhythm three times. Play it softly first (whisper), then loud (speak), and then very loud (shout). Class, echo Emil's phrase by clapping it.
- Mary, let's hear your name played on the triangle. (Mar-y Mock-o-witch) Play it two times, softly.
- Class, echo by snapping your fingers.
- Group leader for row 1, get the box of instruments and give each person in your row a triangle. Row 1, remember where you are to place the triangle when you get it.

Follow the same procedure for distributing instruments to the rest of the class.

- Triangles only will play on Mary's phrase. All instruments will play on Emil's phrase. Which phrase shall we play first? Shall we repeat any? Shall we add another phrase? Are the phrases of the same length? Shall we play some soft and some loud?
- You handled your instruments very well today. Group leaders, please collect the instruments.
- You have worked very hard. Here is one of your favorite records. Let's sit back and enjoy it. You've earned it!

ASSESSMENT 2   The following teaching procedure illustrates some ways to control and modify inappropriate behavior in a chorus rehearsal. How many ways can you identify? Support your reasoning.

Materials   "Gonna Build a Mountain" (page 170, record 2)
Recorders
Rhythm instruments
Resonator bells, xylophones, and other mallet instruments

Concept   A melody may be performed in a variety of styles.

Objectives   1. (Primary) Plan an effective way to perform "Gonna Build a Mountain" in an assembly program.
2. (Secondary) Watch the conductor.

Gon - na build a moun - tain From a lit - tle hill.

Gon - na build a moun - tain, Least I hope I will.

Gon - na build a moun - tain, Gon - na build it high.

I don't know how I'm gon-na do it, On - ly know I'm gon-na try.

Procedure
- Jason, will you read our two objectives for today?
- Let's sing the song, and as we sing, be thinking about how you would like to perform it at the assembly program.
- Last time you sang this song you got lots of compliments on it. Let's list all the ways we might perform the song and then choose the ones that work best. (Play recorders, sing in unison, sing in parts, play a percussion accompaniment, play an Autoharp accompaniment, play bells, add a dance, etc.)
- As usual you have wonderful ideas. Which idea would change the tone color? (Adding instruments)
- Which idea would change the texture? (Singing in harmony, adding an Autoharp accompaniment) Any other changes? (Changing tempo, dynamics)

Have students work in groups to try out their suggestions. Choose the suggestions that are approved by most of the class.

- We can have an exceptionally good performance *only* if every one of you remembers to *watch the conductor*. As we practice this time, I am going to try to surprise anyone who is not watching by slowing down, speeding up, cutting off, putting in holds, and so on. Jean and Tom will keep score and count the number of times you miss the conductor's signal. Let's mark the chart.
- Good! You are improving with every rehearsal!

ASSESSMENT 3 Whenever a problem arises in a classroom, there are many courses of action open to the teacher. Study the following situations and decide how you would handle each one. Be prepared to defend your solution. Compare your solutions with those of others in the class.

SITUATION ONE

The class comes running down the hall and into the music room. Some children bang on the piano as they pass it. Three children go and look out the window. One child sits down and starts to read a library book.

SITUATION TWO

The lesson is going very well. Two children in the back of the room begin to whisper. They are not bothering anyone.

SITUATION THREE

The teacher has tried every kind of song, and yet only about half the class will sing.

SITUATION FOUR

Most of the students are responding well. Suddenly a fight erupts in the front of the room, very near the teacher.

SITUATION FIVE

The teacher constantly has to remind the children to sit up straight. They are always in a slumped position, which is detrimental to their singing.

SITUATION SIX

One student suddenly throws a book across the room. When the teacher tells the student to go to the office, the student refuses.

SITUATION SEVEN

Every time the teacher changes activities, the children begin to talk. As a result, no one can hear the teacher's directions.

SITUATION EIGHT

Whenever the teacher asks a question, the entire class shouts the answer.

ASSESSMENT 4 What would you say to a fifth-grade class to implement the following idea? How would you manage the class to avoid confusion?

Materials "Shoeflies" (record 1)

Concept Most popular music has a steady beat.

Objective Respond rhythmically and creatively to the steady underlying beat.

Procedure **FANCY STEPS**

Have the class keep time to the steady beat of "Shoeflies" by using some fancy steps — strutting on the first beat of each measure and adding a different movement on the third beat. Here are some suggestions.

Snap fingers.	Swivel on one foot.
Clap hands.	Slide free foot outward.
Raise shoulders.	Kick free foot.
Raise hands.	

Now have students plan a movement that combines two or more fancy steps.

10 *Evaluating Learning*

Describe at least three means of evaluation, contrast formative and summative evaluation, and explain the role of grading in evaluation.

In any school system, everyone — the superintendent of schools, the parents, even the students themselves — evaluates the educational program. In some subject areas, evaluation is comparatively uncomplicated. The amount of material learned, the kinds of skills developed, the effectiveness of the teaching, the progress of the students — all can be evaluated objectively by means of teacher-prepared or standardized tests. Parents and teachers can compare a student's test scores with his or her scores on previous tests or with the average scores for the class to determine how the student is progressing. The principal can use test scores to help evaluate the effectiveness of the teachers. The superintendent can use test scores to evaluate the strength of the math program, for example, as compared with math programs in other systems throughout the state or the country.

But evaluation has not been such a simple matter in music, for music is a subjective art and there are many aspects of it that do not lend themselves to objective testing. The student may evaluate the music program on the basis of the variety and appeal of the activities; the teacher may evaluate the music program in terms of the progress students make; the principal may evaluate the music program on the basis of the teacher's ability to maintain discipline during the music period; the parents may evaluate the music program on the basis of one public performance; and the superintendent may evaluate the music program on the basis of hearsay.

Since much of the program must be evaluated on the basis of what is seen and heard, it is possible that some of the evaluations may not be valid. They may be based on such things as discipline or on parents' comments about how nice the children looked on stage, and have nothing to do with the musical worth or the educational goals of the program. In order to determine the validity of an evaluation, it is important to know what is being evaluated.

WHAT CAN BE EVALUATED IN THE MUSIC PROGRAM?

Any aspect of a music program can be evaluated; however, if the evaluation is to be valid, it must be made on the basis of the goals and objectives of that aspect of the program. If, for instance, the principal decides to evaluate the progress of a general music class that has spent six lessons learning about string instruments, the evaluation will be valid only if it recognizes progress in terms of what the students have learned about the instruments' tone color and range, their use in the orchestra and in quartets, and so forth. If the evaluation were made in terms of the students' ability to play the instruments, it would be worthless, since this has not been a goal of the lessons.

Since the goals and objectives of a music program are so essential to a fair evaluation of the program, it is imperative that they be stated clearly. Chapter 4, "Planning Instruction," discusses in detail the many factors the teacher must consider in setting realistic goals and objectives. It is sufficient to say here that in order to evaluate children's musical progress and the teacher's effectiveness, goals and objectives should be written for the program, for instruction, and for the lesson. The discipline of writing objectives nearly always results in better teaching, because the teacher takes the time to think about what students are doing and why.

WHO EVALUATES THE MUSIC PROGRAM?

After the teacher, the most constant and most critical evaluators of the music program at all levels are the students. Children are quick to communicate their feelings about a lesson; they show whether or not they are "with" the teacher by their body posture, facial expressions, attention, and verbal response. When goals are achievable and everyone's progress toward them is considered important, children usually respond positively.

Besides the classroom teacher and the students, those who visit the classroom periodically — the music teacher, the principal, the music supervisor — evaluate the music program in the classroom. Of these visitors, perhaps the music teacher is the only one who will come to the classroom on a regular basis and therefore have an opportunity to make a continuous evaluation of progress. The principal and the music supervisor may have to base their evaluation on as few as three visits a year.

Parents, too, evaluate the music program, often basing their evaluation on a single event. Their evaluation of not only the music program but the total educational program of the school is frequently based on what they witness at the annual spring music festival, since this is the only part of the school program that many of them see.

WHAT ARE SOME OF THE MEANS OF EVALUATION?

Much of the evaluation of any music program is subjective. Although a subjective evaluation is not very scientific, it may not be an entirely inappropriate means of evaluation, because it deals with feelings, just as music deals with feelings.

If it were possible to get honest answers to the question "How do you feel about the music program?" those answers might give a very good indication of how the music program is doing. It is probably on this basis as much as on any that administrators decide whether to expand the music program and whether to approve budget requests.

A more specific but still subjective means of evaluating the music program is the teacher's self-evaluation. Concerned teachers ask themselves questions such as, "What did my students learn today?" "Are the children more interested in music now than they were a month ago?" "How many students are signing up for orchestra or chorus?" "Do the children hurry to get ready when it's time for music?" "Do the children hate to see the music lesson end?" "Do many children raise their hands to leave the room during the music class?" "Do the students offer to help pass out the music books?" When such questions are answered honestly, they can serve as an effective means of self-evaluation.

If an audio or video tape recorder is available, the teacher might try taping a lesson as an aid to self-evaluation. It may be helpful to ask another teacher or the principal or music supervisor to help evaluate the taped lesson.

As another means of self-evaluation, the teacher might have students "take over" the class to review what was taught in the previous lesson. It is amazing how many of the teacher's unconscious habits and mannerisms the students will reflect as they "teach" the class.

Students should be encouraged to do some self-evaluating, too. An audio or video tape recorder can be a valuable tool in helping students evaluate their progress in music.

Teachers should also encourage the students to evaluate their work without the help of electronic aids. They can help the students make judgments about their progress by asking questions that are very specific; for instance, "When we sang 'Crescent Moon' yesterday, we took a breath in the middle of the third phrase. Did we sing the phrase in one breath today?" Such questions help the students focus their attention on one specific event in the music so that they can make a valid judgment about that event.

Some teachers maintain a music profile for each student in the class. The profile consists of a folder for records of all the assessment tasks students have completed, all the contracts they have fulfilled, all the public performances they have been a part of, and any other information that is pertinent. Music profiles provide an objective means of evaluating student progress. They should be shared with both the child and the parents.

Another objective means of evaluating musical progress is with published tests. The most widely-used of these are the Music Achievement Tests. The MAT series helps the teacher determine how well each student has mastered the auditory objectives of the music program by measuring skills such as — pitch discrimination, interval discrimination, and meter discrimination. The tests are available with recordings and answer sheets. They can be administered and scored by the music teacher or by the classroom teacher. National norms have been established for the test results; this constitutes a milestone for testing procedures in music.

Another testing program is the *Silver Burdett Music Competency Tests*, developed as a part of the total *Silver Burdett Music* program to provide systematic evaluation of students' progress. The criteria for the tests were established by the objectives of *Silver Burdett Music*. According to the author, Richard Colwell,

"Most of the questions involve the students' aural perception of the expressive qualities of music: rhythm, melody, form, tone color, texture, tonality, and dynamics. Aural perception is basic to the development of most musical skills and concepts. In addition to the questions on aural perception of basic musical qualities, other competencies examined are:

1. Recognition of sameness or difference in musical style
2. Perception of more than one element within a single composition
3. Recognition of relationships between musical sounds and notation
4. Recognition of specific qualities in the arts."[1]

These tests fill a void in criterion-referenced measurement for elementary school children and provide a unique opportunity for administrators, teachers, and students to evaluate individual progress in comprehending the aural aspects of music. If the objectives of a particular music program are substantially the same as the objectives on which the *Silver Burdett Music Competency Tests* are based, these tests can be used in measuring students' achievement.

WHEN SHOULD THE TEACHER EVALUATE PROGRESS?

Evaluation must be a continuous part of the educational process. The teacher must evaluate every part of every lesson, for what is achieved in each class will affect the next day's lesson plan and may require a revision of the short-range and long-range plans. This continuous (or formative) evaluation is vital to progress, since it enables you to keep abreast of the students' level of skill and understanding. With this procedure you are able to plan lessons that are not boring because they are too easy, or unattainable because they are too hard. Formative evaluation provides you with the knowledge that is necessary to plan and enables you to revise your plans to meet the needs of children realistically.

Summative evaluation requires you and your students to look back over a period of time and measure progress against long-term goals and objectives. Usually this measurement is in the form of a written test. Formative and summative evaluation are both vital to the progress of students and teachers.

WHAT IS THE ROLE OF GRADING IN EVALUATION?

Some school systems have replaced the traditional report-card method of reporting to parents with periodic parent-teacher conferences. The teacher makes an appointment to meet with the parents of each child in order to discuss the child's progress. If the teacher has maintained a music profile for the child, the parent-teacher conference provides an ideal opportunity for sharing it with the parents.

Some schools provide a check-mark system for reporting to parents. In this system of reporting, music activities are listed on a report card. Next to each activity are three boxes under the headings *Regularly, Sometimes, Never*. The classroom teacher or the music teacher puts a check mark in the appropriate box to indicate the extent of the child's participation in each activity. This type of reporting seems fair because it gives the student an objective "grade" based on observable behavior. While participation is not all there is to music education, and while it doesn't necessarily indicate a level of achievement, the child who participates usually has some interest in music and usually benefits from participation. The check-mark system provides an honest report to parents.

---

[1]Richard Colwell, *Silver Burdett Music Competency Tests: Teacher's Guide* (Morristown, N.J.: Silver Burdett Company, 1979), p. 3.

Some kinds of grading can be damaging to students. Teachers who give everyone in the class the same grade indicate to students that they are viewed as a collective entity, not as individuals. Teachers who grade on the basis of behavior are being unfair because a child's poor behavior may be the result of the teacher's unpreparedness, or the teacher's sarcastic attitude, and may have nothing at all to do with music. Teachers who grade on the basis of written work alone are using an inappropriate means of evaluation. Music is an aural art — and aural perception, not written description, should be the heart of the music experience.

Many music teachers teach as many as five hundred students each week. It is difficult to know the level of achievement of each student and give an accurate measurement of progress. If traditional grades are to be given, some means of individual measurement must be used.

GENERALIZATIONS

The following generalizations may be drawn from the discussion of evaluation.

Goals The teacher must evaluate progress in terms of established goals and objectives. The more clearly they are stated, the more accurately progress can be measured.

Process The teacher must continuously evaluate the means of reaching goals and objectives to make certain that the process is contributing to the achievement of goals and objectives, not hindering it.

Awareness Teachers must be observant. They must be aware of students' facial expressions and body posture. They must listen to what students say.

Objectivity Teachers must be objective. They should not make excuses for themselves or for their students. They should neither exaggerate nor rationalize.

Tools Teachers should know the tools of evaluation and use them. They should keep abreast of new developments in the area of evaluation.

Self-Evaluation Teachers should evaluate their efforts honestly, and they should encourage students to evaluate their own progress honestly as well.

Evaluation Formative evaluation is part of every lesson, every day. Summative evaluation is important as a way of gauging progress over a longer period of time. This is especially important in concept development.

Summative Evaluation Summative evaluation is important as a way of gauging progress over a longer period of time. This is especially important in concept development.

ASSESSMENT 1 Study the following quotes and identify the generalization(s) that each typifies. Give reasons for your choices.

1. Teacher: "We've been working on dynamics, phrasing, and diction. Which of them still needs the most work?"
2. Teacher: "I've asked Mr. Wilson to come and hear us sing today."
3. Student: "Hi, Miss Jones! Are we going to have music today?"
4. Teacher: "Close your books and see if you can sing 'Sing Hallelu' from memory."

5. Teacher: "Your folder is on the shelf. Be sure to give yourself credit for learning the Autoharp chords for 'Old Joe Clark.'"
6. Parent: "That was the best PTA program we've ever had!"
7. Teacher: "Look at the objective for today's lesson on the chalkboard. Did we achieve it?"
8. Teacher: "John has been making progress this term in playing the recorder. At the beginning of the term he was far behind the rest of the class, but in the last six weeks, he has improved immensely."

ASSESSMENT 2   Describe a fair and honest method of grading elementary school children in music.

ASSESSMENT 3   Explain the difference between formative and summative evaluation.

ASSESSMENT 4   Discuss the merits and shortcomings of at least three means of evaluation.

11 Important Influences on Music Education

CHAPTER OBJECTIVE   Contrast the Dalcroze, Kodály, and Orff approaches to music education, and describe the influence of the Contemporary Music Project and the Manhattanville Music Curriculum Program on music education.

CURRENT APPROACHES TO MUSIC EDUCATION

In recent years, more and more educators have come to discover the importance of music in the total development of the child. The realization that children can experience the aesthetic impact of music only to the degree that they can perceive the inner workings of music has led to ever stronger pleas to make the school music program more than a continuous sing-along, and to ever more conscientious attempts to find better approaches to teaching children how music works. As a result, different approaches to music education are currently being tried throughout the country. Some of these approaches have found more favor in certain parts of the country than in others. Some of them require that the teacher have special training, usually in the form of workshops leading to certification. Some recommend the use of specially designed instruments or other equipment. Some of them are adaptations of European approaches to music education; some have been entirely developed in this country. The following are descriptions of some of the approaches currently in use.

DALCROZE EURYTHMICS

Dalcroze eurythmics is an approach to music education developed by the Swiss musician Emile Jaques-Dalcroze (1865–1950). Eurythmics consists mainly of bodily response to music that is improvised at the piano. It requires attentive listening, for as the music sounds, the students respond with appropriate body movements. At first, responses are simple — tiptoeing to high, light music; running to fast music; and so forth. As the students' ability to hear contrasts in music becomes keener, the music changes back and forth between light sounds and heavy sounds, fast sounds and slow sounds, connected sounds and detached sounds. Sometimes the class is divided into two groups. One group is instructed to respond to the rhythm that the teacher is playing with the right hand while the other group responds to the rhythm of the left hand.

Eventually, all students learn to respond to two different rhythms simultaneously. For instance, the students may clap in response to a quarter-note rhythm and at the same time run in response to an eighth-note rhythm. As the students' ability to listen becomes keener and they grow in their ability to respond creatively to the music, instruction in music reading and dictation is added.

Ideally, instruction in Dalcroze eurythmics should begin at age four or five. However, it can begin at a later age. Some colleges and conservatories offer courses in eurythmics.

THE KODÁLY METHOD

The Kodály Method, as used in American schools, is an adaptation of a method of music education developed by the Hungarian composer-educator Zoltán Kodály (1882–1967). In Hungary the Kodály Method has had an enormous impact on music education and has resulted in an incredibly high degree of musical literacy among people in every walk of life. It has been effective in developing not only fine performing musicians but appreciative audiences as well.

Beginning at about age three, children are taught singing and rhythmic games. The material for much of the instruction is Hungarian folk music. Using the "sol-fa" system of syllables developed in England by John Curwen, the first songs taught contain only the two tones of children's natural chant, sol-mi. Gradually, children progress to songs that have three tones (sol-mi-la) and proceed in this manner until all the tones of the pentatonic scale have been learned. Eventually, the fourth and seventh tones of the major scale are added.

Part-singing is introduced early in the program, and all singing is done without instrumental accompaniment. As the children sing, they use a set of hand signals also developed by Curwen, with a different hand signal for each tone of the scale.

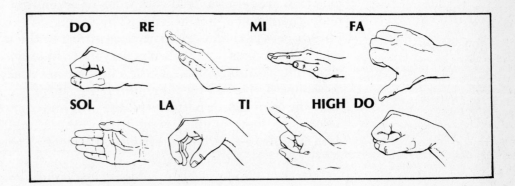

In the Kodály approach, there is a different hand signal for each tone of the scale.

In addition to singing with "sol-fa" syllables, the children practice rhythms by using rhythm syllables. Quarter notes are called "ta," eighth notes are called "ti," and so forth. After the children have had much practice with rhythms and have learned many songs by rote, they are introduced to music reading. They begin by "reading" songs they already know.

The Kodály Method has been successfully adapted for children in this country (see Bibliography for references). Many colleges and universities offer summer workshops in the Kodály Method, some of which lead to certification.

THE ORFF APPROACH

The American adaptations of the Orff approach to music education are based on a program developed by German composer-educator Carl Orff (1895–1982). The Orff approach was originally intended for use with adults in gymnastics and movement classes. The special instruments that are used with the program were originally designed so that students could improvise their own accompaniments for their dances and routines. Eventually, Orff was persuaded by the Bavarian Radio to adapt his approach for use with children.

The Orff approach to music education is too loosely structured to be called a method. It begins with simple rhythms. Children chant words, such as the names of flowers, trees, and birds, in duple and triple meters. They improvise simple sound patterns, using four basic body movements — clapping, snapping, Patschen (slapping the thighs), and stamping. They use these four movements to respond to simple and then gradually more complex rhythm patterns, at first by echoing patterns that the teacher improvises and later by improvising rhythm patterns of their own. As children gain facility in echoing and improvising rhythm patterns, the echo activity develops into a rhythm canon (like a round), and the improvising may take the form of a rondo (ABACADA, for example). The children also use the four body movements to accompany their chants and songs.

After the children have had a great deal of practice echoing and improvising rhythm patterns through movement, they add melody to the rhythm by using the Orff instruments. The melodic Orff instruments include a variety of glockenspiels, xylophones, and metallophones in various registers from bass to soprano. The instruments have metal or rosewood bars that are removable so that when children first learn to play they can make their music "mistake-proof" by taking off the bars they don't need. Early work on the instruments is confined to the tones of the pentatonic scale. This makes it possible for everyone to improvise at the same time, for when only the tones of the pentatonic scale are used, there are no extreme dissonances. Eventually, the children learn to play and improvise ostinatos (melodic or rhythmic patterns played over and over) on the instruments to accompany their singing. In addition to these "mallet" instruments, children may also use recorders, string instruments, and a variety of drums and other percussion instruments.

In the Orff approach, emphasis is on creative improvisation. Musical literacy is emphasized only to the extent that it enables the children to write down their improvisations or the patterns they play to accompany songs so that they can remember them and play them again at another time.

Carl Orff's program of music instruction is contained in *Orff-Schulwerk: Musik für Kinder* (Mainz, Germany: B. Schott's Söhne). It has been translated into many languages, including English. (Publications in English are listed in the Bibliography.) Many colleges and universities offer summer workshops in the Orff approach, some of which lead to certification.

OTHER INFLUENCES

The Contemporary Music Project (CMP), funded by the Ford Foundation through the Music Educators National Conference (MENC), has influenced music education since 1959 in at least two ways. CMP promoted the use of contemporary music in school music programs by placing young composers-in-residence in school systems where they composed music for performing groups. In addition the project sponsored workshops and experimental programs to encourage music teachers, students, and college professors to compose as a way of learning about and applying techniques used by contemporary composers; to listen to a wider variety of music; and to explore the components of music, such as pitch, duration, and timbre.

The Manhattanville Music Curriculum Program (MMCP), funded by the United States Office of Education, has had an impact on music education since 1965. MMCP focused on four principle ideas: (1) Exploration and discovery should be the primary means of learning. (2) All types of music should be studied without bias. To this end, the concept approach was used. This included inherent concepts, such as melodic direction or dynamics, and idiomatic concepts, such as the I, IV, V harmonies often found in American folk songs. (3) Contemporary music should be the source of most of the study material. (4) Students should assume the roles of composer, conductor, performer, and critic, so as to experience music from the viewpoint of each. This would provide greater insight into the nature of music.

The Contemporary Music Project and the Manhattanville Music Curriculum Program have had an influence on both the content and process of music education. Many of their ideas are now an accepted part of music education, even though workshops and seminars are no longer sponsored by either group.

ASSESSMENT

1. In what ways are the Dalcroze, Kodály, and Orff approaches to music education similar? How are they different?

2. In what ways are the Contemporary Music Project and the Manhattanville Music Curriculum Program similar? How are they different?

3. Of the five approaches discussed, which one do you feel has the most validity? Why?

4. Which of the five approaches do you feel are the most important to the future of music education? Why?

12 *Why an Education in Music?*

The arts are among humanity's most potent creations. They are the means through which human beings can rise above the level of daily existence and give that existence a dimension beyond the purely utilitarian. Without the arts, people cannot convey to successive generations the wide range of feelings — from joy to despair — that characterizes human experience.

There is no culture, however remote or primitive, that does not have music in some form as a part of its ethos. It is obvious that any creation as universally pervasive as music must be an important life force. Any education that deals with events that are of a dynamic nature must therefore include music as one of the fundamental human manifestations to be studied.

In creating a work of art, whether it be a cave painting, a folk song, or a theatrical tragedy, the artist idealizes the emotional content of experience in order to communicate to others a shared sense of human feelings. When they experience the art work, people living hundreds of years after the moment of creation can comprehend, to a greater or lesser degree, these idealized emotions.

Of all the arts, music is the most abstract. It communicates no overt message through precise words or photographic pictures. Rather, music is a phenomenon that relies on a threefold response for its reception. The first is a physiological response to the stimulus of sound waves: music is heard. The second response is intellectual: the mind perceives that the sound is music rather than thunder or a train whistle, and that some "events" are taking place in the music — the music is loud or soft or it is "moving" fast or slow. The sophistication of the intellectual response depends primarily on the degree of training the listener has. The third response is psychocultural: the music stimulates in the listener a feelingful response to the musical events. At the same time the music may stimulate a feelingful response that is the result of enculturation — sadness, joy, or patriotism, for example — that society has decreed are appropriate responses to particular kinds of music in the culture.

Enculturated responses, although learned, do not constitute an education in music. Rather, enculturated responses are formed as a result of simple observation of others' responses to sound stimuli. Music triggers reactions that the child learns are appropriate in the culture. Without an organized and structured education in music itself, the child's responses will always be narrow, culturally biased, sparse, and haphazard.

Education is a process whereby the learner comes to grips with the intricacies of the environment and begins to expand the horizons of his or her personal life space. In fact, education cannot be considered complete unless it includes some form of reaching out to environments that are not within the local sphere of the learner. Most elementary education starts with those events and things closest to the child's personal knowledge; as the child grows, the sphere is expanded to include other places and things with which the child can have no personal contact.

THE CHILD'S EDUCATION IN MUSIC

From birth, the physically "normal" infant reacts to several basic stimuli — sound, light, color, and movement. These are the elements from which are derived much of what constitutes the arts. In music, a baby reacts to the loudness and softness of sounds, the steadiness of beats, the smoothness of melodies.

Music education begins with songs and activities that interest the child through the "subject" of music: animals, parents, games, holidays. Music education also begins to call attention to the events in music itself with which the child is acquainted: moving fast versus moving slowly, sounds that are loud versus those that are soft, and many other qualities that are readily apparent. As the child matures, the emphasis on what is happening in the music begins to take precedence over the meanings of words in the music. The words in a song are obvious; the musical events are more subtle. The gradual growth in understanding musical events that are more and more subtle constitutes education in music. A child cannot achieve this kind of education without being taught.

When teachers deal with those questions that concern themselves with how music works rather than with home, pets, and family, they are dealing with music concept-building. A student can be taught to build concepts about music just as he or she has already probably begun to build concepts about his or her enculturated responses to music. Conceptual responses are in the form of categorization, classification, and sorting — the choosing of one solution to a musical problem over the several alternatives available.

The more involved the student becomes with the workings of music itself, the greater will be the ability to make value judgments about it — judgments based on an understanding of the music's construction. The broader the kinds of music he or she is exposed to, the greater the likelihood that horizons will be expanded and that he or she will be able to cope with styles that are totally unfamiliar. When this stage is reached, it is almost a certainty that the student will be able to deal with music intelligently and independently, and be motivated to do so.

MUSIC EDUCATION METHODOLOGY AND STRUCTURE

The degree to which children are motivated to develop concepts about music depends largely on the method that is used in the presentation of instructional materials. The presentation must be made in such a manner that the student's interest is captured and retained long enough for the concepts to form in the mind of the student. The teacher of music must create an atmosphere in which learning is not inhibited by boredom. Music, by its nature, evokes the use of entertainment as an interest-building device. Entertainment, when used as a means rather than an end, is one of the prime psychological aids to learning. Singing games, percussion play, folk dances, humorous songs are all part of the musical heritage and should be included in the learning process. However, the teacher does a disservice to the student if he or she does not utilize the interest in these activities for concept-building — for learning why a particular composition sounds the way it does, how it is put together, how it is like or different from some other kinds of music.

Throughout the text, the authors have attempted to show that music instruction can proceed in a clearly-defined educational structure. A child learns about any subject matter when he or she is ready to learn about it — and not before. Therefore, knowledge of child growth and development is an essential prerequisite for the development of a plan for education in music. In addition, the discipline of music itself presents structures for learning. For example, it is impossible to teach the concept of subdivided beat unless one is assured that the concept of beat itself is internalized by the student beforehand. It becomes mandatory, therefore, to combine knowledge about child growth and development with knowledge about the structure of music and how it works in organizing any music instruction program.

MUSIC EDUCATION AS AESTHETIC EDUCATION

When the student is able to think effectively about music concepts, he or she is in a position to deal knowledgeably with a personal value system. These value judgments about music are then based upon an understanding of the passage through time of musical events and a feelingful response to these events. In addition, these value judgments are predicated upon exposure to a wide variety of music and activities — much wider than can be attained through casual cultural acquisition.

The goal of any education program in music must be the continuous and lifelong development of informed taste. The teacher of music has a personal goal for the students: that they should continue to desire contact with the art form for the rest of their lives.

APPENDIX

MUSICAL CONCEPTS

The following chart indexes by page number the concepts that are dealt with in the teaching procedures throughout *Teaching Music*. These are representative of concepts that should be included in the elementary music program, but no attempt has been made to be prescriptive or inclusive. Published music textbooks or school curriculum guides serve that purpose well. Some teachers may wish to use the procedures as they are written, others may adapt them, and still others may use them as a point of departure. The authors' intent is to explain and illustrate the teaching of concepts by presenting many specific examples.

	6- and 7-Year-Olds	7-, 8-, and 9-Year-Olds	9-, 10-, and 11-Year-Olds
Beat	1		28, 171
Rhythm Patterns	6, 74, 127	13	
Meter	74	21	
Duration		13, 59	
Silence	104		
Tempo	98		28, 117
Melody	74, 127	17, 132, 163	32, 89, 93
Tonality			135
Phrases	127	167	
Form	74, 160		47, 94, 117
Tone Color	4	114	
Texture			41, 62, 106
Style			139, 147, 169

HINTS FOR TEACHING ROTE SONGS

1. In the sample strategy that introduces "All Around the Kitchen" (page 2, record 1), attention is focused on the words of the song when students are asked to act them out. Students hear the song repeatedly as they play the game. Nonetheless, if good singing is expected, it is almost certain that it will be necessary to isolate some phrases for extra practice. Improving the singing can best be accomplished when attention is concentrated solely on singing, without engaging in other activities, and when the singing is unaccompanied.

2. In the sample strategy using "Somebody's Knocking at Your Door" (page 4, record 1), students are required to listen to the song a total of four times, with their attention focused on specific words and on the sounds of different instruments. They may have the song generally in mind, but they will probably need to have their attention directed to the words and melody before being able to sing it well.

   To discover how much students remember, ask which words were sung more than once. If no one can answer, there is good reason for listening to the song again. Ask students to sing only the repeated words ("Somebody's knocking at your door"). If the melody of the next phrase ("O, Joshua, why don't you answer?") is sung inaccurately, isolate and practice it. When those three phrases are sung well, try singing the entire song. Isolate and practice any phrase that most students are singing poorly. When singing without the recording, be sure to give the beginning pitch and some clear signal (drop your hand or nod your head, for example) to show the exact moment when students are to begin singing. Remind students to assume a comfortable but upright posture as a preparation for singing.

3. In working with "Sing Hallelu" (page 6, record 1), students hear the song several times and will probably remember the tune, but they will need help if both verses are to be mastered. Work for clear enunciation by having students speak the words. A visual reminder in the form of pictures of key words is an effective aid to memory.

4. "I'm Gonna Sing" (page 9, record 1) is a short song with few words and much repetition; therefore, students are asked to listen to the whole song, rather than break it into parts. For each of the suggested listenings, students are given a specific purpose or a specific way to respond. Most students can sing this kind of song when presented in this fast-paced manner. However, always be alert to students' inaccuracies and poor diction, and correct them before they become habits. A song learned inaccurately is almost impossible to correct, and sloppy diction detracts from the character and meaning of the song.

5. The suggestions for teaching "All Night, All Day" (page 11, record 1) require students to listen to the whole song four times, each time for a specific purpose. Since the focus is on the mood and meaning of the words, most students should be able to sing it after these four listenings. If not, isolate and practice poorly sung phrases. Do not accept breathy, dead singing as soft singing. Remind students to maintain good posture. Model well-articulated consonants, especially when singing softly. Be

particular about getting ready to sing and beginning together. This is achieved by insisting on eye contact with students. "Ready" should be a signal to sit tall and look at you.

6. You may play the recording of a song such as "Love" (page 24, record 1) in order to motivate students to learn to sing it. Phrasing is especially important in a song such as this. Hence, teaching it phrase by phrase is one way to emphasize, and work on, good phrasing. Model correct musical phrasing. Help students feel the rise and fall of each phrase, and the movement toward the climax within each phrase. Be sure that phrase endings are held for their full value.

GENERALIZATIONS

Listening Students need to listen to a song a minimum of three times before being asked to sing. Focus attention on one thing for each listening.

Practice Practice singing without other activities and without accompaniment. Isolate and practice portions of the song as needed.

Whole Song Many songs are easily mastered by hearing the whole song. Others require a phrase-by-phrase approach. Students often learn to sing a song by hearing it used as an accompaniment for other learning activities.

Model Give students a good model. Model accurately, with attention to musical phrasing, dynamics, good diction, etc.

HINTS FOR TEACHING MUSIC READING

1. As an aid in performing and eventually reading rhythm patterns, many successful teachers associate words with note values. For example, in "Sambalele" (page 14, record 1), a rhythm pattern is taught with words from the song. Durations and rhythm patterns can also be associated with movement, with counting, and with rhythm syllables.

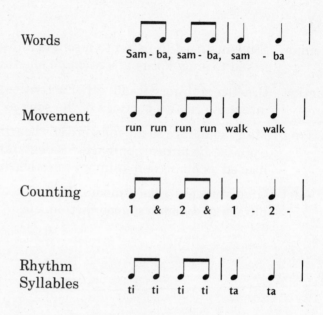

2. Successful teachers seize every opportunity to develop musical literacy, and they use many methods. Most methods take into account the following broad guidelines.

   a. Start with the sound.

   b. Interpret the sound with movement or chanting.

   c. Represent the sound with symbols such as these.

   d. Represent the sound with standard notation.

   e. Read the notes.

   f. Sing the notes at sight.

3. Resonator bells can be used to give students many opportunities to associate pitches with the corresponding notation. When they have mastered the rhythm of a song, an ostinato, a phrase, or a pattern, they can practice independently on bells and learn to play at their own rate.

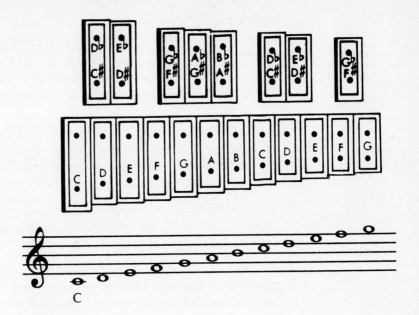

HINTS FOR TEACHING LISTENING

1. Keep in mind three guidelines in planning listening activities: experience, purpose, and response.

    a. Listening is more effective when it can be related to knowledge and experience. When children listened for the rhythm of "Coranto" (page 16, record 1), for example, they had already sung, chanted, and clapped rhythm patterns.

    b. The listener's attention should be focused on one specific thing. In "Coranto" the teacher asked students to listen specifically for a repeated rhythm pattern.

    c. The listener should be required to respond in a way that will make it clear to the teacher whether or not the purpose of the listening has been accomplished. In the example, students were expected to clap the pattern and then arrange visual materials to match the sounds.

2. Avoid situations in which background music is played while children work on other things. In these situations children form the habit of "tuning out" the music.

3. To help children achieve the goal of a particular listening experience, play the music more than once. Let students know that they will have more than one opportunity to hear the music. Establish a climate of concentration without a feeling of stress.

HINTS FOR TEACHING MOVEMENT

1. Growing bodies need to move, and discipline problems can often be avoided by taking care of this need. Some teachers plan at least one activity that requires movement in each thirty-minute lesson.

2. Successful movement activities require space and the physical setting is important. When working in a large room (a gymnasium, for example), students should be given time to explore the area. Each student should find his or her "space" for moving freely without bumping into anyone or anything. Some classrooms can be rearranged to provide extra space by placing the chairs and desks against the walls or in one section of the room.

3. If space is limited, allow individual students or small groups to take turns moving. Students can also stand beside their desks and mark time in place, or engage in some axial movement such as bending or stretching.

4. Prior to the start of a movement activity, establish definite sound cues that will tell students when to start and when to stop. Insist that they obey the signals every time. Sound cues, such as a single stroke on a gong, are often more effective than verbal instructions.

5. Dances or other movement activities that require special foot patterns can be taught first by using the hands on the legs or in the air in front of the body, then by moving the feet while still sitting, and then by actually performing the steps.

HINTS FOR TEACHING RECORDER

1. Plan a step-by-step introduction to the instrument, such as the following.

   HOLDING THE RECORDER
   Hold the recorder with both hands, the left above the right. Place the thumb of the left hand on the thumb hole, which is on the underside of the instrument. Put the first (index), second, and third fingers of the left hand on the first three holes at the top of the instrument. Put the first, second, third, and fourth fingers of the right hand on the bottom four holes. Let the thumb of the right hand support the instrument from underneath. When playing, lift all fingers from the holes except those needed for each note.

   COVER-THE-HOLE TEST
   Press just hard enough so that the hole makes a light mark on each finger and on the thumb of your left hand.

   MAKING A SOUND
   Cover the tip of the mouthpiece with your lips. With only the thumb and index finger of the left hand in place, blow gently through the recorder. Start the sound with "doo." You will be playing B.

2. Provide a fingering chart so that students can practice individually.

   RECORDER FINGERING CHART

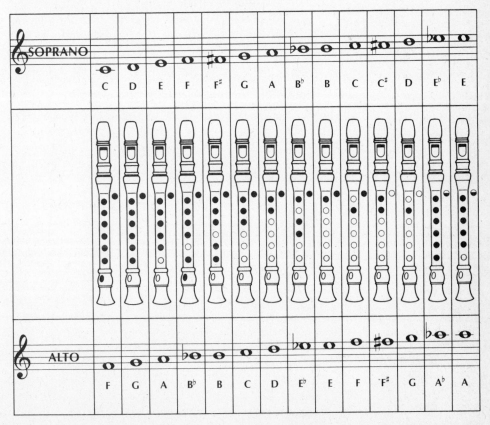

1. The Autoharp is a classroom instrument that offers the student almost instant success in playing a chordal accompaniment. To play an accompaniment for "Wade in the Water" (page 39, record 1), for example, have the student use three chords: D minor, G minor, and A_7. The buttons for these chords are adjacent to each other and fall easily under the index, middle, and ring fingers of the left hand. Have the student cross the right arm over the left and strum with the right hand.

2. Most beginners need to be reminded to keep a chord button depressed for as long as they want the sound to last.

3. Provide for short periods of practice so that students can develop coordination in pressing the chord buttons and strumming the strings.

4. Encourage students to experiment with various kinds of strumming techniques: away from the body (low to high), toward the body (high to low), and pluck-strum (pluck a low string near the body and strum away from the body on the next beat).

For songs in triple meter, students can use the pluck-strum technique, changing the pattern to pluck-strum-strum.

5. When younger students begin to play the Autoharp, they can practice in pairs, one student pressing the chord buttons and the other strumming the strings.

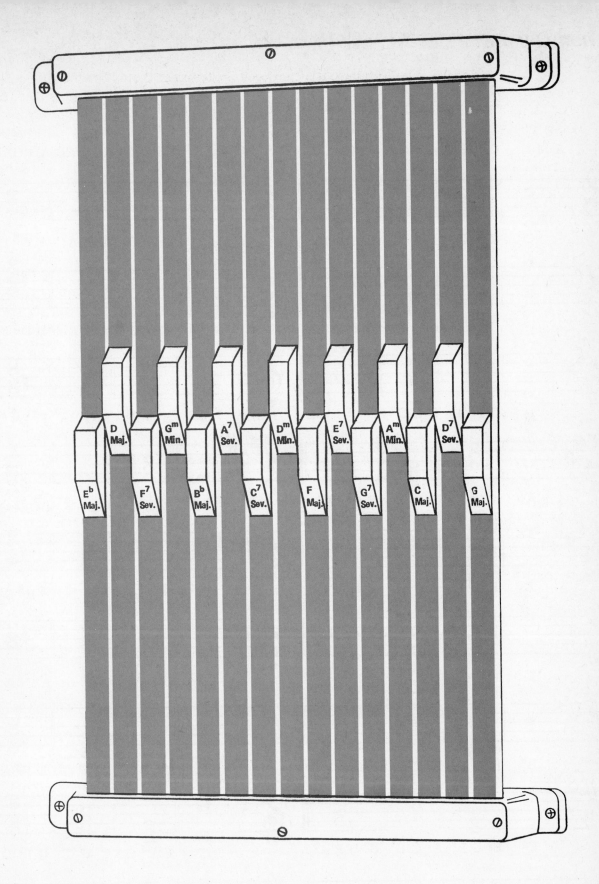

CHORD CHART

THEORIES OF CHILD GROWTH AND DEVELOPMENT

This is a brief outline, not intended to be exhaustive. For additional information, see the Bibliography.

STAGE THEORISTS

Stage theorists believe that children progress through stages of physical and maturational development. **Arnold Gesell** was one of the first stage theorists; he described major areas of behavior, based on physical maturation. Since many musical skills are essentially dependent on physical development, this early work should not be ignored. Here is a brief outline of Gesell's theory:

Six- and seven-year-olds
Show fatigue easily
Are susceptible to respiratory diseases
Become restless if asked to sit still too long
Enjoy large muscle activity
Have difficulty with fine motor control
Like to manipulate objects
Can follow specific directions
Can work in a small group for short periods of time

Eight- and nine-year-olds
Enjoy strenuous muscular activity
Have increasing skill in fine motor control
Are more cooperative as members of a group
Will rebel if authority is oppressive

Ten- and eleven-year-olds
Show a marked difference between early and late maturers
Tire easily after vigorous activity
Differ individually in ability to comprehend, remember, and reason
React in a generally favorable manner to reasonable authority
Manifest inner turmoil through aggressive, silly behavior or day dreaming

Jean Piaget, a foremost proponent of the stage theory, believed that cognitive development comes about when the learner reaches the necessary maturation level. Piaget developed an elaborate structural system, based on the stage theory, that extends from birth to adulthood. Very briefly, here is the outline:

Birth to eighteen months
The sensorimotor stage
Adapts and acquires motor skills

Eighteen months to seven years
The pre-operational stage
Refines motor skills
Is egocentric
Is unable to generalize

Seven to twelve years
The stage of concrete operations
Is able to reason
Understands quantity in any form
Can sort objects
Needs to deal with the concrete by touching and feeling
Cannot readily generalize

Twelve years	The stage of formal operations Is able to think in the abstract Understands cause-and-effect relationships Can make moral judgments Piaget believed that a child can learn only that which he or she is mature enough, or ready, to learn.

Jerome S. Bruner is classified by some as a stage theorist because he also identified stages of development. This is a brief outline:

Early infancy	The enactive stage Experiences are stored almost unconsciously
Infancy and toddlerhood	The stage of iconic representation Experiences and objects are stored in a visual representational form
Preschool	The stage of symbol representation Experiences and objects are stored and represented abstractly or symbolically (as in language)

Bruner differed from Piaget in believing that ideas, knowledge, or problems could be presented in a form simple enough to be understood by *any* learner. He did not believe in maturational readiness. He believed that readiness could be taught. For this reason, Bruner has sometimes been classified as an information-processing theorist: he believed that the learner does not just learn units of information but learns how to program or process them, and that older children process that which is to be learned in a different manner than younger children.

LEARNING THEORISTS

Learning theorists believe that cognitive development comes about when the learner experiences and observes, associates, reinforces, and responds to different situations repeatedly, and finally generalizes and transfers that which has been learned to other situations. This increases the ability to think independently and to handle more complexities. **Robert M. Gagné** described this kind of hierarchy, for any age, as follows:

Steps in learning	Signal learning Stimulus/response learning Chaining Verbal association Multiple discrimination Concept learning Rule/principle learning Problem solving

One very important agreement among all the theorists has been that children grow and develop best in a stimulating environment.

BIBLIOGRAPHY

Current School Music Texts

Boardman, Eunice, and Barbara L. Andress. *The Music Book, K–8,* New York: Holt, Rinehart & Winston, 1981.

Crook, Elizabeth, Bennett Reimer, and David S. Walker. *Silver Burdett Music, K–6.* Morristown, N.J.: Silver Burdett Company, 1981.

Marsh, Mary Val, Carroll Rinehart, and Edith Savage. *The Spectrum of Music, K–8.* New York: Macmillan Company, 1980.

Reimer, Bennett, Mary E. Hoffman, and Albert McNeil. *Silver Burdett Music, 7–8.* Morristown, N.J.: Silver Burdett Company, 1982.

Music in the Elementary School

Beall, Gretchen H. *Music as Experience: Structure and Sequence for the Elementary School.* Dubuque, Iowa: William C. Brown Company, Publishers, 1981.

Bergethon, Bjornar, and Eunice Boardman. *Musical Growth in the Elementary School,* 4th ed. New York: Holt, Rinehart & Winston, 1979.

Gillett, Dorothy. *Comprehensive Musicianship Through Classroom Music.* Menlo Park, Calif.: Addison-Wesley Publishing Company, Inc., 1975.

Hackett, Patricia, Carolynn Lindeman, and James Harris. *The Musical Classroom: Models, Skills and Backgrounds for Elementary Teaching.* Englewood Cliffs, N.J.: Prentice-Hall, Inc., 1979.

Knuth, Alice Snyder, and William E. Knuth. *Basic Resources in Learning Music,* 2nd ed. Belmont, Calif.: Wadsworth Publishing Company, 1973.

Newman, Grant. *Teaching Children Music: Fundamentals of Music and Method.* Dubuque, Iowa: William C. Brown Company, Publishers, 1979.

Nye, Robert, and Vernice Nye. *Music in the Elementary School,* 4th ed. Englewood Cliffs, N.J.: Prentice-Hall, Inc., 1980.

Raebeck, Lois, and Lawrence Wheeler. *New Approaches to Music in the Elementary School,* 4th ed. Dubuque, Iowa: William C. Brown Company, Publishers, 1980.

Swanson, Bessie R. *Music in the Education of Children,* 4th ed. Belmont, Calif.: Wadsworth Publishing Company, 1981.

Music Education for Early Childhood

Andress, Barbara L. *Music Experiences in Early Childhood.* New York: Holt, Rinehart & Winston, 1980.

_____. *Music in Early Childhood.* Washington, D.C.: Music Educators National Conference, 1973. (MENC now located in Reston, Va.)

Simons, Gene M. *Early Childhood Musical Development: A Bibliography of Research Abstracts, 1960 –1975.* Washington, D.C.: Music Educators National Conference, 1978. (MENC now located in Reston, Va.)

Music Education for Exceptional Children

Beer, Alice S., and Richard Graham. *Teaching Music to the Exceptional Child: A Handbook for Mainstreaming.* Englewood Cliffs, N.J.: Prentice-Hall, Inc., 1980.

Hardesty, Kay W. *Silver Burdett Music for Special Education.* Morristown, N.J.: Silver Burdett Company, 1979.

Nocera, Sona D. *Reaching the Special Learner Through Music.* Morristown, N.J.: Silver Burdett Company, 1979.

Dalcroze, Kodály, Orff

Choksy, Lois. *The Kodály Method: Comprehensive Music Education from Infant to Adult.* Englewood Cliffs, N.J.: Prentice-Hall, Inc., 1974.

————. *The Kodály Context.* Englewood Cliffs, N.J.: Prentice-Hall, Inc., 1981.

Daniel, Katinka. *Kodály Approach: Method Book One,* 2nd ed. Champaign, Ill.: Mark Foster Music Company, 1979.

Landis, Beth, and Polly Carder. *The Eclectic Curriculum in American Music Education: Contributions of Dalcroze, Kodály, and Orff.* Washington, D.C.: Music Educators National Conference, 1972. (MENC now located in Reston, Va.)

Mark, Michael L. *Contemporary Music Education.* New York: Schirmer Books, 1979.

Orff, Carl, and Gunild Keetman. *Orff-Schulwerk: Music for Children,* Vols. I –V. Translated by Doreen Hall and Arnold Walter. Clifton, N.J.: European-American Music, 1978.

Regner, Hermann, ed. *Music for Children,* Vol. 2 (*Orff-Schulwerk,* American ed.). Schott Music Corporation, 1977. (Distributed by European-American Music, Clifton, N.J.)

Zemke, Sr. Lorna. *The Kodály Concept: Its History, Philosophy, Development,* 2nd ed. Champaign, Ill.: Mark Foster Music Company, 1977.

Learning Theory, Philosophy, Psychology

Blakeslee, Thomas R. *The Right Brain: A New Understanding of the Unconscious Mind and Its Creative Powers.* New York: Doubleday & Company, Inc., 1980.

Bruner, Jerome S. *The Process of Education.* New York: Vintage Books, 1961.

Gordon, Edwin E. *Learning Sequences in Music Skills, Content and Patterns.* Chicago: G.I.A. Publications, 1977.

Gowan, John, and E. Paul Torrance. *Creativity: Its Educational Implications,* 2nd ed. Dubuque, Iowa: Kendall/Hunt Publishing Company, 1981.

Hilgard, Ernest, ed. *Theories of Learning and Instruction.* Chicago: University of Chicago Press, 1964.

Madsen, Charles H., and Clifford K. Madsen. *Teaching Discipline: A Positive Approach for Educational Development,* 2nd ed. Boston: Allyn & Bacon, Inc., 1970.

Madsen, Clifford K., and Charles H. Madsen, Jr. *Experimental Research in Music.* Raleigh, N.C.: Contemporary Publishing Company of Raleigh, 1970.

Mager, Robert F. *Developing Attitude Toward Learning.* Palo Alto, Calif.: Fearon Publishers, 1968.

————. *Goal Analysis.* Belmont, Calif.: Fearon Publishers, 1972.

————. *Preparing Instructional Objectives,* 2nd ed. Belmont, Calif.: Fearon Publishers, 1975.

————, and Peter Pipe. *Analyzing Performance Problems, or You Really Oughta Wanna.* Belmont, Calif.: Fearon Publishers, 1970.

Meske, Eunice Boardman, and Carroll Rinehart. *Individualized Instruction in Music.* Washington, D.C.: Music Educators National Conference, 1975. (MENC now located in Reston, Va.)

Miel, Alice, ed. *Creativity in Teaching.* Belmont, Calif.: Wadsworth Publishing Company, 1961.

Monsour, Sally. *Music in Open Education.* New York: Center for Applied Research in Education, Inc., 1974.

Reimer, Bennett. *A Philosophy of Music Education*. Englewood Cliffs, N.J.: Prentice-Hall, Inc., 1970.

Sanders, Norris M. *Classroom Questions: What Kinds?* New York: Harper & Row, Publishers, Inc., 1966.

Savary, Louis M., and Margaret Ehlen-Miller. *Mindways: A Guide for Exploring Your Mind*. New York: Harper & Row, Publishers, Inc., 1978.

Child Growth and Development

Ambron, Sueann. *Child Development,* 3rd ed. New York: Holt, Rinehart & Winston, 1981.

Angrilli, Albert, and Lucile Helfat. *Child Psychology*. New York: Harper & Row, Publishers, Inc., 1981.

Bloom, Benjamin. *Human Characteristics and School Learning*. New York: McGraw-Hill Book Company, 1976.

Bruner, Jerome S. *Toward a Theory of Instruction*. New York: W.W. Norton & Company, Inc., 1968.

Gagné, Robert M. *The Conditions of Learning*. New York: Holt, Rinehart & Winston, 1965.

Gesell, Arnold, Frances Ilg, and Louise B. Ames. *The Child from Five to Ten,* rev. ed. New York: Harper & Row, Publishers, Inc., 1977.

Havighurst, Robert J. *Human Development and Education*. New York: David McKay Company, Inc., 1953.

Jackson, Nancy Ewald, Halbert B. Robinson, and Philip S. Dale. *Cognitive Development in Young Children: A Report for Teachers*. Washington, D.C.: U.S. Dept. of Health, Education and Welfare, 1976.

McCandless, Boyd, and Robert J. Trotter. *Children: Behavior and Development,* 3rd ed. New York: Holt, Rinehart & Winston, 1977.

McKinney, Fred, Melvin Zax, and Raymond P. Lorion. *Effective Behavior and Human Development*. New York: Macmillan Inc., 1976.

Mead, Margaret. *Growing Up in New Guinea*. New York: William Morrow & Company, Inc., 1976.

Piaget, Jean. *Science of Education and the Psychology of the Child*. New York: Penguin Books, 1976.

Pulaski, Mary Ann. *Understanding Piaget,* rev. ed. New York: Harper & Row, Publishers, Inc., 1971.

Roedell, Wendy C., Ronald Slaby, and Halbert B. Robinson. *Social Development in Young Children: A Report for Teachers*. Monterey, Calif.: Brooks/Cole Publishing Company, 1977.

Zimmerman, Marilyn P. *Musical Characteristics of Children*. Washington, D.C.: Music Educators National Conference, 1971. (MENC now located in Reston, Va.)

Tests and Measurement

Colwell, Richard. *The Evaluation of Music Teaching and Learning*. Englewood Cliffs, N.J.: Prentice-Hall, Inc., 1970.

_____. *Music Achievement Tests*. Chicago: Follett Educational Corporation, 1969.

_____. *Silver Burdett Music Competency Tests*. Morristown, N.J.: Silver Burdett Company, 1979.

Gordon, Edwin. *Musical Aptitude Profile*. Boston: Houghton Mifflin Company, 1965.

Mager, Robert F. *Measuring Instructional Interest, or Got a Match?* Belmont, Calif.: Fearon Publishers, 1973.

INDEX

Accompanying
   as a learning device, 10–11, 15, 16, 18, 21, 23, 25, 34–36, 40, 43, 48, 49, 59, 63, 75, 77, 79, 89, 95, 105–106, 119, 129, 148, 164, 165, 170
   as a teaching tool, 3, 7, 10, 52, 56, 99
Activities
   chanting, 14, 49
   creative, 63, 79, 95, 97, 116, 117, 160, 168
   involving dramatizing lyrics, 2, 116
   involving music reading, 15, 16, 18, 20, 23, 25, 26, 40, 59, 75, 81, 90, 96, 97, 119, 164
   involving playing instruments, 3–5, 9–11, 15, 16, 18, 21, 23, 25, 26, 33–36, 38, 40, 43, 48, 49, 52, 56, 63, 75, 77, 79, 82, 89–91, 93, 95, 97, 105, 106, 119, 128, 129, 132, 137, 148, 161, 164, 165, 169, 170. *See also* Instruments.
   movement, 1–3, 10, 18, 24, 52–53, 57, 59, 63, 79, 99, 118, 119, 128, 170, 171
   singing, 3, 7, 8, 10, 11, 15, 18, 20, 21, 29–32, 34, 36, 43, 45, 48, 49, 56, 59, 62–64, 74, 75, 79, 82, 95, 98, 105, 107, 108, 115, 116, 119, 128, 129, 132, 147, 148, 168, 170
   using games, 82
   using large groups. *See* Large group activities.
   using motions, 3, 7, 8, 14–18, 20, 22, 23, 26, 29–31, 49, 50, 59, 62, 63, 79, 82, 90, 95, 97, 98, 105, 106, 118, 128, 133, 138, 160, 161, 163, 164, 167–169
   using small groups. *See* Small group activities.
   using visual aids, 15, 17, 23, 26, 51, 56, 57, 95
Activity packets, learning. *See* Learning activity packets.
Aesthetic education
   methodology in, 183–184
   music education as, 184
Autoharp
   activities using. *See* Instruments.
   diagram, 193
   hints for teaching, 192
   parts for. *See* Parts for classroom instruments.

Beat. *See* Musical concepts.
Behavior. *See* Discipline.
Bells. *See* Resonator bells.
Bongo drums. *See* Instruments.
Bruner, Jerome S., 196

Chanting, activities involving. *See* Activities.
Child growth and development, theories of, 195–196
   Bruner, Jerome S., 196
   Gagné, Robert M., 196
   Gesell, Arnold, 195

   Piaget, Jean, 195
Classroom instruments
   activities using. *See* Instruments.
   parts for. *See* Parts for classroom instruments.
Claves. *See* Instruments.
Cognitive skills
   analyzing, 92, 96
   categorizing, 48, 92, 96
   comparing, 96
   conceptualizing, 4, 92
   contrasting, 96
   describing, 48
   differentiating, 5
   discriminating, 48
   evaluating, 96
   generalizing, 96
   labeling, 48
   recalling/remembering, 5, 91, 96
   recognizing, 6
   synthesizing, 92, 96
Composing, as a classroom activity, 149–152
Computer software, 139
Concepts, musical. *See* Musical concepts.
Contemporary Music Project (CMP), 181
Creative activities. *See* Activities.
Creativity, 144–156
   as a means of learning, 149–152
   generalizations on, 153–154
   importance of, 152–153
   through inventing, 144–146
   through making new combinations of musical elements, 146–149
Curwen's system of *sol-fa* syllables and hand signals, 179

Dalcroze eurythmics, 178–179
Deductive approach to teaching, 92–93
   generalizations on, 96
   used with inductive approach, 94–96
Discipline, 157–171
   controlling inappropriate behavior, 162–165
   establishing mutual respect, 157–158
   generalizations on, 167
   modifying inappropriate behavior, 165–166
   preventing discipline problems, 157
   setting limits of behavior, 158–162
Dramatizing lyrics, activities involving. *See* Activities.
Drums. *See* Instruments.
Duration. *See* Musical concepts.

INDEX OF SONGS AND LISTENING SELECTIONS

Songs

Listening Selections

ISBN 0-382-05867-4

SILVER BURDETT COMPANY

80 20P 00
ISBN 0-382-05867-4